HARRIET BEECHER STOWE

This is the story of Harriet Beecher Stowe, author and philanthropist, and it is spun in this most beautifully written and affectionate biography. Winifred Wise tells us of Hattie's girlhood in a house full of children, and of Lyman Beecher, her father, lovable but rigidly Calvinistic. From the early days, Hattie loved to read and indulge her natural talent for writing. Throughout most of her life, including her marriage, there was a lack of money. But with the unbounding success of *Uncle Tom's Cabin,* Hattie entered the limelight. She was now rich with living and rich with achievement.

This book is a warm tribute to a great woman who portrayed the whole background of what today is called the civil rights movement. Thus Hattie Beecher comes vividly out of the past and into the present.

Harriet Beecher Stowe

WOMAN WITH A CAUSE

By

WINIFRED E. WISE

G. P. Putnam's Sons

New York

CONTENTS

HARRIET BEECHER STOWE

1

BEECHER'S DOZEN

HATTIE BEECHER could not remember when she had learned to read, or when she had not been rummaging through the barrels of old sermons in the big airy garret at the top of the parsonage. The musty smell of the papers intrigued her childish fancy; and as she spelled out titles whose meanings were as unintelligible to her as Choctaw, she felt in touch with worlds that were far beyond her understanding.

She was small for her age and could barely see over the tops of these barrels that held so many thousands of her father's words and thoughts and thundering warnings of the fate that awaited the sinners who nodded below his pulpit on Sunday mornings, afternoons, and evenings in the hard square pews of the old meetinghouse. Which barrel should Hattie tip over today? It was always a question for her to decide on any one of the hundred afternoons of her childhood when the grownups were too busy to bother with her, or her brothers had gone fishing.

Left to find her amusements, she sought them in curious ways that would not have occurred to any other member of her large and lively family. Who but Hattie would have cared to wade around among papers fretted with mildew and odorous with damp so that even the mice ignored them when they built their cozy nests?

Hattie had no hint of the treasure that awaited her—and her alone—when, on one momentous afternoon, a brightly colored book slid down the paper avalanche and landed at her feet. It was a tattered copy of the *Arabian Nights* that somehow had found its way into a household where the Bible supplied the chief reading matter and which viewed New England as the center of the universe. Hattie fell upon it with the eagerness of a child starved for beauty and color and romance as her imagination took flight upon a magic carpet to the jewelled and perfumed court of the Sultan of the Indies.

The volume was hers, she thought as she clutched it to her breast—"finders keepers"—and no one should take it away from her. She would read it over and over again, soaring, too, upon the clouds of her own fancy.

It was many years later when—with almost the same ecstatic surprise and unbelief with which she had discovered this book in a barrel—she suddenly found herself famous. It happened, almost literally, overnight with the publication of her astonishing first novel, *Uncle Tom's Cabin*. Out of the struggles of the years and out of her own heart and soul, she had produced the most powerful and influential book of the nineteenth century and one of the most-discussed novels of all time. To her—the wife of an impecunious professor and the mother of seven—it was as though she had rubbed the lamp of Aladdin and dripped riches untold through her hands.

Hers was an almost childlike marvel that the book in

which she had expressed herself so passionately concerning the evils of slavery was an immediate and sensational success. Who was this Harriet Beecher Stowe? Within a few weeks after publication, the question was on thousands of lips throughout America and shortly in the British Isles and France. How could an obscure and unknown author— and a woman at that—have skilfully produced characters that walked right out of her pages and spoke for themselves? What sort of person was she? Behind the story of *Uncle Tom's Cabin* were the days and the years of little Hattie Beecher, scarcely five feet tall even when she was grown, but casting a very long shadow that many said hastened the great Civil War.

No such excitement attended her birth on June 14, 1811 in Litchfield, Connecticut, and even her name was a hand-me-down. There had been an earlier Harriet who had died in infancy, and Harriet Elizabeth also inherited her cradle and her swaddling clothes, since nothing in the parson's household could afford to be wasted—not even the affections of her parents, which had to cover five other living children and would encompass many more. Including Lyman Beecher himself, there would in time be a full "Beecher's dozen." The Reverend Beecher was later to become known as "the father of more brains than any other man in America," but folk were apt to forget that Roxana was the mother of the most distinguished among them.

Hattie's parents were both of old New England stock long settled in Connecticut. For her time, Roxana was well educated and of more liberal thought than Lyman, who had met her during one of his summer vacations from Yale. He was educating himself largely by his own industry, but with some assistance from an uncle who had taken him into his home as an infant, following the death of his mother. From his father, a well-read New Haven black-

smith who paid slight attention to his son, Lyman inherited a powerful physique and the driving force that would
make him use his pulpit like an anvil.

Harriet Elizabeth was in the middle of the Beecher
brood and thus she remained—an in-between known
more familiarly and endearingly as Hattie. She had arrived
at a time when babies were no novelty in the crowded
Beecher household, but must be tucked away somewhere
to grow up more or less by themselves until the Rev. Lyman Beecher might have individual concern for their
souls.

Gentle mother Roxana cuddled and coddled her baby,
indulging Hattie along with the rest of the brood that
weighed heavily upon her slender shoulders, but finding
few hours to spare them. She kept boarders, and the result
was that the old white frame house was always threatening
to burst at the seams—like the minister's scant salary of
only eight hundred dollars a year. Visiting ministers came
with their families and, as was the custom, often stayed on
for weeks. Along with two young colored girls in the
kitchen and a washerwoman who came once a week, Roxana was sore pressed to discharge all her duties. Besides, as
the parson's wife she had "to keep up appearances," since
the Beechers were numbered among the leading families
of what was often called the most beautiful village in Connecticut.

Roxana had a sympathetic confidante in the wife of the
eminent Judge Reeve, whom Hattie always remembered as
the largest woman she had ever seen. She stood in awe of
the portly woman who emerged almost daily from her
chaise to divert her mother from the humdrum by sharing
with her the higher realms of thought and an appreciation
of Roxana's paintings and her cobweb embroideries.
Somehow Roxana still found time to execute a few of these

here and there; she had always found time . . . somehow . . . some days.

A cultured woman, Roxana cared for the beautiful
things of life that the grinding years with Lyman Beecher
so often denied her—as, later, life with Calvin Stowe would
deprive her daughter Hattie. They were both like flowers
seeking a foothold in the hard New England soil.

And yet, even as a tiny child Hattie sensed the warmth
that flowed between her father and her mother. They were
still in love, and they adored each other. During his ardent
courtship of Roxana Foote, Lyman had admitted that he
had a temper quick to heat and quick to cool. It cooled
most often when Roxana was near him. He was the most
unruly of her children, the one with the loudest voice, the
most erratic and the dearest. (Hattie never forgot her
mother through the rest of her life, nor did Lyman and the
others.) In any emergency, she was always there, "quiet as an
angel from above."

(Nor did Hattie wish to escape the memory of her exquisite Aunt Mary Hubbard, her mother's sister, whose experiences in the West Indies became a part of family legend)
Some dark mystery—revealed to Hattie only later when she
was able to understand it—had caused her aunt to die "of a
broken heart," though others laid it to consumption. Aunt
Mary had lived with them, and Hattie's mother had cried
over her endlessly. The infection had gone deep.

As a tiny girl, Hattie was not concerned with grown-up
affairs and tragedies, but she could see her mother standing
in the nursery door and proclaiming in her sweet voice,
"Remember the Sabbath day, children, and keep it holy."

And she could recall, always, her mother's distress over a
childish bit of mischief. Exploring a closet, Hattie had
found a paper bag containing what looked like onions and,
with her smaller brother Henry Ward—later to be one of

America's most famous preachers—had eaten them. They had tasted odd and sweetish, and feeling sick, the children had run to their mother. When told what they had done, she looked so sad that Hattie would have preferred to be whipped. They had eaten up the choice tulip bulbs which Mother's seafaring brother, Samuel Foote, had brought all the way from Holland to indulge her love of what was beautiful and rare.

Mother never switched them, but she could make a child feel worse than Father ever did. It was Father who was the family disciplinarian, and he taught them early that obedience must be immediate, unquestioned, and cheerful. "Mind your mother . . . go wash your face . . . stop whining." The quince tree beside the house supplied all the twigs necessary to enforce Father's sharp commands.

It was almost impossible not to forgive this quixotic man who, when in the mood for it, could be the liveliest of playmates. Coming home of a Sunday evening after the last of the three Sabbath sermons which, hours long, raised him to a peak of nervous tension, he would relax and regale the children by playing lively tunes on his fiddle—*Go to the Devil* and *Shake Yourself*. Sometimes he would seize Catherine as a partner and dance jigs all the way round the kitchen. Catherine, his first-born, was eleven years older than Hattie and destined to become a pioneer in woman's education; she was always Lyman's favorite and the butt of a humor that at times could be boisterous. Once their father had plunged Catherine fully clothed into a washtub full of water simply to watch her reaction.

He was an unpredictable man, was Lyman Beecher, and the electricity of excitement hovered always about him. When Father entered the door, all the household was aware of it and snapped to attention. It was impossible to appear dull in his presence without Lyman's calling attention to it—as he often did with Hattie, embarrassing her when she was silent by asking whether the cat had run away with her tongue. The Reverend Beecher performed best before an audience, and he was seldom without one, either at home or in the world outside.

Though Roxana was usually in the background, she was the family balancewheel, accepting with little question whatever her impractical husband brought home to her. It could be an orphan girl who was to live with them until her marriage, or an impoverished clergyman seeking a new appointment, or even a bale of cotton such as her husband had bought at a bargain soon after their wedding day. Puzzled as to what use to make of this gift, Roxana concluded to spin it, have it woven into a carpet, and ingeniously paint it with a pattern of flowers. Thus a garden bloomed even in winter upon the floor of the simple Long Island cottage that had been their first parsonage.

Roxana had an amazing capacity to use her wits and "make do" which led also to her starting a school in this East Hampton home. Like many another woman of her time, but with far more imagination than most, Roxana tucked in here and padded there to make her home attractive and fill out the gaps in their income. Quiet and unobtrusive, Roxana might dream of luxuries but never admit that she longed for more than her nimble wit and fingers could supply.

As Hattie grew up, she was to follow along a similar path and more and more to resemble her mother. Like Roxana, she was soft and feminine, delicate of feature, and shy in the presence of strangers. Yet Hattie in addition was possessed of the fiery Beecher spirit which, smouldering always behind a deceptive façade, was to blaze into a talent that would rocket her forever from obscurity.

During her lifetime, Roxana was a warm shelter from

the winds of puritanical chill and the harshness of theological discipline that threatened to envelop all of them in
the years that lay ahead. Without her, Lyman would feel
like a child suddenly left out alone in the dark; and Hattie
would grow up as best she might without a mother's love
to caress her and fill the void in her heart.

Hattie was only five when she lost her, but Roxana's
memory was enshrined. It was as though her presence
lingered like the afterglow of the sunset in which Roxana
had had a vision and a premonition of death. She was riding out with her husband one mid-August evening when
she shivered and told him calmly and without hysteria that
she had caught a glimpse of heaven and knew that she was
not long for this world. She spoke with such conviction
that her husband did not attempt to reassure her; if it were
a foolish fancy, it would pass. If not, he had no fear for the
immortal glory of one who had been an angel upon earth.

Accepting what could be inevitable, he left her to make
a week-long journey on clerical business and returned to
find his household in turmoil. Rushing up the stairs to his
wife's bedside through a cluster of frightened children and
members of his congregation offering prayers, he burst
into tears. Death was coming swiftly for Roxana, and the
primitive medical science of the time was helpless to avert
it. Little was known about the nature of tubercular infection, and no precautions had been taken when Roxana,
two years previously, had nursed her sister Mary. The fateful infection had been running through her body; and
now, in her early forties, she was dying of "galloping consumption."

When Hattie went out into the road, the stage driver
pulled to a halt to ask how her mother was. Farmers called
after her, and the shelves of the pantry were crowded with
delicacies sent in by the countryfolk to tempt her mother's

appetite. Once every day Hattie was permitted to go in and see her. Propped up in bed, her mother seemed already far away from earthly cares and from the eight children who stood weeping about her—Catherine holding baby Charles while William, Edward, and Mary as the next eldest tried to comfort George, Hattie, and Henry.

Soon the night came when Lyman Beecher knelt at her bedside and, holding his wife's hand in his as though he could not bear to let her go, repeated in a voice that reverberated through the house like the notes of an organ: "Ye are come unto Mount Zion, the city of the living God, to the heavenly Jerusalem . . ."

Stirring in her sleep, Hattie saw the fair face of her mother with flushed cheeks and a quiet tender smile on her lips. Mother must be well again, and Hattie awoke to shout aloud in a transport of joy. Then an adult came in to hush her and to tell her that her mother was dead.

The September day when they buried her mother was a bleak one for Hattie, though she was too young to understand all about it: the funeral, the walking to the burial ground, the sobs of the mourners dressed entirely in black. Where had Mother gone, and why would she never return?

Father said she was in heaven, but how could she get there from the ground in which they had buried her? Drawing Hattie to her, the old Negro washerwoman, Candace, kissed her hand while the tears fell upon it. It was three-year-old Henry who put two and two together from the talk of the grownups and darted out of the door. Soon he was seen lugging a heavy shovel from the barn and industriously digging a hole. Lest he get his black mourning frock dirty, Catherine went out to stop him, only to discover what he had in mind. "I'm going to heaven to find Ma," he lisped with all his childish earnestness.

Hattie sought no such active outlet for her own bewil-

dering sense of loss. She lay staring into the dark after
Catherine kissed her tenderly and snuffed out the candle,
feeling cold and lonely until Henry crept in beside her.
Stroking his golden curls, she held him close. The two of
them would always cling together, for each needed someone to love.

2

TO GUILFORD

Everywhere in the creaky old house Hattie saw reminders of her mother: the furniture she had adorned with painted decorations; the pictures of birds and flowers skilfully rendered with her artist's brush; the portrait miniatures upon ivory; the fine black lace which Hattie had watched her make on little bobbins. On every hand the plainness and austerity of the parsonage were relieved by the tasteful touches of a mother who was nowhere to be found.

Wandering about disconsolately, Hattie soon was brought up short by brisk Aunt Harriet Foote, her mother's sister for whom she had been named. Aunt Harriet had been nurse through the fatal illness and now was preparing to return to Nutplains, the family home at Guilford. Packing her portmanteau for the return journey, Aunt Harriet was including her niece's clothing and small possessions, for she was taking Hattie with her. The child was too sensitive to be allowed to remain brooding about the house here in Litchfield, and she would be a comfort to her grief-stricken grandmother.

Aunt Harriet and Aunt Esther Beecher, Lyman's half sister, had decided this between them, barely asking her father's permission. Now that Roxana was not here, he seemed too dazed by his loss to care what temporary disposition might be made of any of his children.

Aunt Esther had moved in from the small house nearby which she shared with Grandmother Beecher to take over the management of the household; and already the two spinsters were beginning to clear out the overloaded closets and shelves and to set things to rights. My, how slack and easygoing the Beechers had been—not to mention names or to speak ill of the dead. Roxana had been a saint, but she had had her faults.

Spinsters with no children of their own to run helter-skelter and leave rooms in disarray could have decided ideas about how families—and husbands—should behave; how neat they must be, and how careful that every article was put to use or stored away from mildew and moths. "Waste not, want not" was the motto, and high time it was put into effect for the Beechers. As for schedule and appearing for mealtimes like clockwork, it would appear that Lyman Beecher had never heard of such nonsense.

Guilford was a long day's journey away, and Hattie had seldom been out of the sight of Mount Tom which, misty and blue in the distance, marked the farthest end of a world bounded by wooded hills and by the flash of rivers and cattail-flanked ponds. She was excited at the thought of boarding one of the stagecoaches which came dashing into the village with a whoop and halloo from the driver that set the dogs to barking and gentlemen hurrying to hear the latest news. The driver brought the mail, collected toothsome gossip, and posed as an authority upon the do-

ings in Washington and Boston and New York. The arrival of a coach was always an event in a village day that
was otherwise placid. The outside world did not matter
seriously to the good folk of Litchfield.

Squeezed in between her aunt, still in mourning blacks,
and another lady in bright rustling silks that smelled
faintly of lavender, Hattie was off to new adventure. From
time to time the two ladies sniffed audibly as smoke from
masculine pipes filled the cramped space in which they
were riding, and Aunt Harriet reached into her reticule
with an ostentatious gesture to draw out the smelling salts.
It was her way of rebuking the uncouth behavior that
ladies must encounter in a public coach, sitting knee to
knee with rough homespun-clad males.

The plumes on Aunt Harriet's bonnet shook with indignation and with the jolting of the coach, while Hattie
tried to peer around her and catch a glimpse of the sights.
What her wide grey-blue eyes could see of the villages
through which they were passing looked very like Litchfield, and she was surprised. This other countryside should
be somehow different, and yet here were the same neat
white fences and ringing blacksmith shops and general
stores with their clusters of loafers that she had known all
her short life, the same white church steeples against hills
that blazed with autumn glory.

At the close of a long and wearying day, they arrived
after dark at a lonely white farmhouse where her grandmother's arms were waiting to envelop her. Burying her
head in Hattie's silky brown curls, the dear old lady wept
silently.

Soon they were having tea at a table set before a great
roaring fire, and Hattie was drinking from a cup not heavy
like the Litchfield crockery, but light as an eggshell. As the
candlelight danced upon the lovely old pieces of silver and

made an aureole of Grandmother's snowy white hair, Hattie was not too shy to admire the large gold ring which she wore. Grandmother must be rich! It was the ring her husband had given her upon her wedding day, Grandmother explained as her sad eyes brightened.

She was a twinkly sort of person, as Hattie was soon to discover; but tonight, as Grandmother rose from the tea table, a solemn mood descended upon the little company. Uncle George had come in from his farm chores to join them and to kneel while Grandmother read from her prayer book, seeking pages that would bring her closer to Roxana. It was, indeed, as though she saw the image of her child of long ago in little Hattie, and her tremulous old voice broke.

Uncle George stepped forward to console her, while Aunt Harriet hustled her travel-worn little namesake off to a big curtained four-poster bed. It had been a day filled with confusion and with new experiences, but here the marvel of them all awaited her. She was to sleep surrounded by draperies of an extraordinary pattern.

Aunt Harriet left a candle in the room so that she would not be frightened of the dark; and now, as she lay in her warm flannel gown, she was free to examine the India linen fabric which her sea captain uncle, Samuel Foote, had loaded upon his sailing vessel during one of his Far Eastern voyages. Mammoth plants twisted and turned in strange convolutions and colors about Chinese pagodas; giant birds pursued odd-looking insects; bells were about to ring over the heads of sleepy-looking mandarins. Hattie could only lie there making up stories about them until she fell fast asleep.

With Grandmother in the next bed and Aunt Harriet beside her, she felt enclosed in the warmth of their love. At home she was only one of many clamoring for attention, but here she was first person singular. Why, the servants called her "Miss Hattie"! Always submerged heretofore, she began to bloom in this only-child atmosphere.

"Pliable as she was to all outward appearances, the child had her own interior world, where all her little notions and opinions stood up crisp and fresh like flowers that grow in cool, shady places," Hattie was to write of a little girl like herself in *Pearl of Orr's Island.* "If anybody too rudely assailed a thought or a suggestion she put forth, she drew it back into this quiet inner chamber and went on. . . . There is no independence or pertinacity like that of these seemingly soft, quiet creatures, whom it is so easy to silence, and so difficult to convince."

In Grandmother's eyes, precocious clever Hattie could do no wrong. Grandmother knew how bored a five-year-old girl might become when set down to sew, and let her run out to play among the scarlet autumn leaves. Whenever she broke a needle or lost a thimble, Grandmother managed some excuse to cover up for her with Aunt Harriet, who had sterner ways of expressing her love for this motherless, pretty child.

According to her views, Hattie's training had been much neglected by her overburdened mother, and now was the time to make up for her lacks. A little girl should be taught to move very gently, to speak softly and prettily, to say "Yes, ma'am" and "No, ma'am." Girls were never to be so animated and boisterous as to make a tear in their dresses, and they were to enjoy sewing and knitting. On Sundays they were to go to church and make all the proper responses; then they were to come straight home without dawdling and be catechized.

Without Grandmother to spoil her at every opportunity, Hattie could have felt herself to be encased in rules as rigid as the whalebone corset which her aunt wore to give

her the proper figure of a woman beneath her petticoats
and pantaloons. Never was a more energetic or well-mean-
ing woman entrusted with the education of a little girl!

Her little cousin Mary, who lived nearby, came over on
Sunday evenings to sit on Aunt Harriet's other knee, while
black Dinah and Harry, the bound boy, stood behind them
that they might benefit from religious instruction. Hattie
had discovered that a grave and solemn voice pleased her
aunt, and accordingly she repeated the Episcopalian cate-
chism. The answer to the first question— "What is your
name?"—was easy. It was so much simpler than the Presbyterian primer at home which asked: "What is the chief
end of man?"

Aunt Harriet was a dyed-in-the-wool Episcopalian, be-
lieving that her church showed the only true way to salvation. In her private heart, she did not even believe that
Lyman Beecher was an ordained minister; and on her visits to them in Litchfield, she always walked past his meetinghouse to attend the little Episcopal church which, to her
mind, was the only place where the gospel was dispensed in
orderly fashion.

She did not express these views directly to Hattie, but
the child had sharp ears to overhear what her aunt said to
others; she wondered what her aunt meant by "uncovenanted mercy." Her aunt was such a forceful figure that
she must know what she was talking about when she remarked that "many persons outside the Episcopalian
church will be saved at last, but they are resting entirely
upon uncovenanted mercy." Was such mercy like a chair
that someone might have the power to pull out from under you?

Hattie was too young to understand much of the theological discussion either here or at Litchfield, and she preferred the evenings when the family gathered to read from

the Bible. Grandmother took such a personal interest in all the apostles that they began to seem like real people to Hattie. The old lady always smiled indulgently over Peter. "There he is again, now," she would say. "That's just like him. He's always so ready to put in."

Grandmother was as blind to Peter's faults as she was to Hattie's. She was so sweet and comfortable, so easy to love, that Hattie's heart overflowed. She never wanted to leave her and go back to Litchfield.

In her secret heart, Grandmother was an old Tory and often took the side of King George when some patriot blamed him for the American Revolution. Opening her Prayer Book, she would read to Hattie the old prayers for the king and queen and all the royal family which had been repeated every Sunday in the churches of colonial times. Here in Nutplains, the Bible and events of past history were as vivid as the family mementoes surrounding her: embroidery and paintings and letters from her lost mother and Aunt Mary, the trophies from foreign shores which Uncle Samuel collected. There were Moorish slippers and ingots of Inca gold, ivory carvings by the whalers, and mats from Mogadore. Hattie had a mind that was always forming pictures; and here, in the quiet of this gracious, well-run home mellowed by a century of living, she could daydream with no noisy boys to interrupt her.

Here, too, she heard her first poetry when Uncle George quoted the ballads of Walter Scott and the verses of Robert Burns, another farmer like himself. To astonish her uncle and delight her grandmother, she memorized two long passages from the Bible and twenty-seven hymns. The sensitive film of her brain would be able to unreel them for the rest of her life. It was the first manifestation of a memory for words, scenes, and conversations that continued to be prodigious. Encouraged by her Nutplains audience, no feat seemed too much for her to accomplish.

Nutplains was so different from Litchfield that they were even to celebrate Christmas. Whatever would her father say? Back home, where the stern traditions of the Puritans held sway, Thanksgiving and the Fourth of July were the only festivities. "There is not a shadow of evidence that the first Christians kept Christmas. It wasn't kept for the first three centuries, nor was Christ born anywhere near the twenty-fifth of December." Those were Lyman Beecher's own words, but Grandmother and Aunt Harriet had no intention of letting them take the joy out of Christmas for Hattie as they had for Roxana.

As Hattie went out into the snowy woods with a carol-singing throng to gather holly and evergreens, her small heart rejoiced. She was in and out of all the preparations, while the house smelled of plum cake and spice. Dinah was bustling from morning till night, and Grandmother and Aunt Harriet were forbidding Hattie to look in the closet where the presents were kept. Christmas presents! "Don't peek" were the magic words that kept her on a tiptoe of suspense.

With the gathering dusk of Christmas Eve, she could hear the runners of sleighs squeaking and crunching over the frozen road and the lively jingle of bells. Everyone was out tonight calling greetings, and when at last they bundled into the cutter and Uncle George picked up the reins, Hattie's heart beat faster than the horses' hooves carried them. Surely, somewhere amongst this skyful of stars must be the star of Bethlehem which Grandmother had told her about, the one which had guided the wise men.

On ahead of them was the little church with its high peaked Gothic windows, every pane sending streams of candlelight across the radiant snow. "Glory be to God on high," sweet and solemn voices were singing, "and on earth peace, good will towards men."

Hattie held tight to her grandmother's hand as they pounded the snow from their boots and moved onward from the vestibule into what must be heaven brought down to earth. Every arch was garlanded in greenery, and above the chancel glittered a great golden star that, to Hattie's dazzled eyes, could have been the very star that had shone over Bethlehem above the Infant Jesus. Her heart filled with love for the Baby and His birthday—truth to tell, she would always prefer Him to God. Unlike His Father, Jesus was not always angry.

She trembled with happiness as she sat there amidst the light of the candles and the intoxicating incense of juniper and pine. "We praise Thee, we bless Thee, we worship Thee . . ." angel voices were singing. It was as though one of them could be her mother's.

As she danced about next morning in the red dress and red slippers that were such a joy after Puritan grey, she discovered another present that was one of the few toys she was ever to receive. A wooden doll with jointed arms and blue glass eyes that stared up at her—oh, wonder of wonders! However her father might deplore the color and pageantry and excitement of Christmas, his little daughter approved of them heartily.

3

PLAIN LIVING AND
HIGH THINKING

Hattie remained in Nutplains almost a year before her absent-minded father sent for her. He was always misplacing his spectacles only to discover several pairs of them high on his forehead, and it is possible that Hattie had been similarly forgotten in the rush of his parish days. "With the best of intentions," neither he nor anyone else at Litchfield would ever have time to give her the solace of love and individual attention or to make her feel that she was more than an insignificant "out-of-place, out-of-form" little person. She was burning with curiosity and a desire to see and hear and know all that interested her elders, as at Guilford; but here at home she was again being told not to talk, or to get out of the way or go to bed. "Miss Hattie" indeed!

Her twelve-year-old sister Mary was helping Aunt Esther in the kitchen, kneading dough for the bread, putting up preserves for the winter, making candles in an endless succession of tasks. As for capable Catherine, she had been assigned the formidable duty of making all of the children's clothes as well as her own. In these days before the invention of the sewing machine, every stitch had to be run up by hand; and often it meant sewing far into the night by the flickering light of wax tapers. Catherine was only seventeen; and with aching head and fingers, she sighed for the riches that allowed more prosperous families to keep a professional seamstress busy. Her mother had never been able to afford one, but with slight help from relatives and parishioners, she had miraculously managed to keep her family decently covered.

How her mother had ever accomplished this chore with seldom a complaint Catherine would never understand. She herself had no intention of being a quiet martyr and not scolding, and she was sharp with Hattie when the little girl shirked her basting and ran off to play. With the appearance of company, Catherine was always ready to put the lid on her workbasket and became a stream of gaiety and mirth.

Those who knew Catherine only slightly were apt to think of her only as a bright, thoughtless, lighthearted girl without a serious care in the world. And it was Catherine who made up verses when occasion required it; the family rather fancied her as an authoress. Catherine was a writer of biblical dramas for school exercises or of doggerel for one of the pet funerals at which Hattie was always chief mourner. "Here lies our Kit," was one epitaph, "who had a fit and acted queer. Shot with a gun, her race is run, and she lies here."

Hovering in the background like the voice of conscience to remind them of duty was Aunt Esther, still insisting, but in vain, on "a place for everything, and everything in

its place." She had put up pegs and hooks so that coats and
pantaloons, shawls and bonnets should conform to the
rules that were blithely ignored. They were shockingly ill-
behaved, she thought; yet somehow the household jolted
along, as households will, until a merciful quiet descended
with the Puritan Sabbath.

Out playing on Saturday afternoons, exploring the
brooks and making dams, Hattie and her brothers hoped
the day would come when the sun never set. Catherine had
told them they must get to liking Sundays, or it would be
bad for them; but ten-year-old George and Hattie didn't
see how anyone could be honestly fond of it. As they made
their way reluctantly back to the house in the gathering
shadows, they prepared to face Aunt Esther and the stern-
faced reminder that with sunset the Sabbath had begun.
No balls, no tops, hoops, or willow-whistles—all must be
handed over as a guard against temptation before each
child lined up in the kitchen for a thorough scrubbing in
the battered tin washtub.

Next morning they were expected to sit in a solemn row
while outside the birds chattered merrily, unmindful of
Sabbath restrictions. Within, all was so silent that they
could hear the tick of the old grandfather clock and the
buzz of the bluebottle flies. Through the door of the front
parlor they could see their father in sober, freshly brushed
Sabbath garb with the spectacles resting upon his prominent nose. His restless blue eyes were scanning the great
Bible spread across his knees as he made last-minute notes
for his sermon; but while Father might be in communion
with God, the restless children felt closer to Satan.

Hattie made faces to tempt the others to laugh; Mary
fussed with her collar; George said he was thirsty and went
out to the well. Thumbing through the primer with its
garishly colored pictures of the garden of Eden and the

reminder that "in Adam's fall, we sinned all," they strained their ears for the sound of the meetinghouse bell. While it would mean going from one prison to another, they would have a ride down the elm-arched streets in the family carryall, and a chance to see who was entering their father's church and who had been wooed away by the Episcopalian upstarts.

Hattie looked forward to seeing old Judge Reeve with his long silvery hair and his gold-headed cane; he always hugged little girls because he said that if they weren't good, they were about to be, where boys were about to be bad. The only thing to do with boys was to thrash them.

To Hattie, the bleak old Presbyterian meetinghouse with its double row of high windows was fully as awe-inspiring as Solomon's temple. She had long hours Sunday mornings and afternoons to observe the grapevine carvings and the fading red tulips painted on either side of the pulpit, while she sat with her sisters and brothers directly beneath her father's high podium. For diversion, the children could speculate upon which of the reverend elders would be first to nod and whether one of the dogs pattering up and down the aisle would today make a response to the sermon. Dogs accompanied their masters to church and on occasion howled.

During the afternoons, the pious church mice provided further entertainment quite outside the order of the Presbyterian service, which at this period was interchangeable with the Congregational. Hattie could see the mice watching bright-eyed from their holes, awaiting a chance to creep out and devour the crumbs left over from the dinner baskets which countryfolk brought to church. When her father rose to one of his peaks and hurled words like "eternal damnation," the little rodents beat a prudent retreat.

It was not until sundown that she herself could escape, if escape there could be.

The iron rod of her Puritan upbringing was always to both strengthen and torment her. From early years she had no rest for her tender little soul. With her father an intensification of the heart and spirit of New England, it could scarcely be otherwise. "Plain living and high thinking" was the rule among the Beechers, and rigid dogma was the mold. They must accept it willy-nilly or revolt from it, and the struggle would shape the history of an extraordinary family. Also, it was soon to win the young Beechers a stepmother of aristocratic lineage.

Called to Boston for a preaching foray against the "blasphemies" of Papists and freethinkers, Lyman Beecher met there a Miss Harriet Porter. She was the niece of the eminent Rufus King, who had been minister to England under Washington and Adams, and she belonged to a group of cousins famed for beauty and cleverness from South Carolina to Maine. Lately, however, Miss Porter had turned her concerns from high society to the state of her soul. Lyman Beecher, strong and sure, seemed the very man to advise one who felt herself to be "an infant in Christ."

While always to remain devoted to the memory of his lost love Roxana, the Reverend Beecher was ever to require a woman at his side to exalt him upon his crusades and to reassure and steady him. He was shrewd rather than ardent as he reviewed Miss Porter's qualifications of charm, grace, and religious devotion. She might well fill the role, he calculated; and within a few days after their first meeting, he asked her to marry him. It had taken him two years to win Roxana's consent, but Miss Porter's response was immediate.

Lyman Beecher was in his forties, but she was well into

her twenties. Though it was high time she was wed, the shabby overcrowded parsonage must have come as a shock to one so gently reared as the former Miss Porter. It was one thing to see Lyman Beecher in Boston as a king among men, and quite another to face the harsh realities of an underpaid preacher's life.

To Hattie and the other younger children, their new mother in her beautiful clothes seemed like a princess, and they stood in awe of her. Even when she took them into her lap and let them play with the rings on her smooth delicate hands, it was hard for them to be friends. Though her voice was sweet, Hattie was not to be easily won. Within a few days the little girl was openly defiant before she turned heel and ran. "You have come and married my Pa. When I grow up, I'll go and marry your Pa."

Hearty country youngsters as all of them were, they felt uncomfortably rude in the presence of their elegant stepmother. She might insist that she loved little children, but Hattie and Henry found her to be distant and cold. Their warm responsive natures longed for tender caresses, and she was never to seem like a mother to them. She was not harsh or cruel, and she did "the office-work of a mother"; but neither was she gay and spontaneous. Truth to tell, it was a rare woman who would not have been overwhelmed by Lyman Beecher and his ebullient eight. Within a few years, one of them was to be recording this glimpse of the family:

Mama is well, and don't laugh any more than she used to. Catherine goes on just as she always did, making fun for everybody. George is as usual. Hattie makes just as many wry faces, is just as odd, and loves to be laughed at as much as ever.

It was their father whom the children idolized, and their father who responded to the lure of the bright autumn days by shouting that it was high time to go nutting. Dumping out the contents of every basket in the house, despite the protests of his wife and Aunt Esther who saw their sewing spilled out on the floor, he led the way through the woods to the chestnut trees and dared the boys to climb higher than he could. Once, shinnying up fifty feet to the first branches of a tree that hung over a precipice, he swung over the abyss to shake down the nuts upon the heads of his marvelling children. In the pulpit or afield, Lyman Beecher was a hard man to beat.

He could even make a game of hard work. Foremost in attack upon the huge family woodpile, he joked and told stories that flew as fast as the axes and chips. Hattie, running about in a little black coat that she thought made her look like one of the boys, helped to stack it. She toiled like one possessed for a day and a half, urged on by the hope that her father would praise her. He was always saying that he wished she were a boy so that he could raise her to be a minister; now she would show him that she could work harder and longer than any of them.

With father at the apple-peeler regaling them with stories, the chore of cutting up apples for sauce made many a family evening a merry one. All around the kitchen fingers flew, while a great brass kettle simmered upon the hearth, filling the air with fragrance of a delicious brew that was to be stored by the barrel and frozen. Sometimes Aunt Esther read from the works of Sir Walter Scott, who had somehow escaped her father's ban against novels.

As Hattie sat there, industriously working away and snug and quiet as a mouse in the chimney corner, she was absorbing each nuance and sound. Now Father's attention was upon Catherine and on William and Edward as he raised questions of theology and, to train them in logic, purposely took the wrong side. When Hattie grew older, she too would be trained in this informal way, and it would find its echoes in *Uncle Tom's Cabin*. Lyman Beecher was honing minds against his own flint, and sparks flew when he pointed out to them where the real arguments lay. "Do thus and so, and you'll trip me up."

Village curfew at nine sent them all off to bed to be up with the dawn for family prayers, breakfast, and chores. If Hattie hurried to finish hers, she might have time to herself after school, when she could hurry off to the woods or hide herself in the garret. Then no one could find her to darn stockings or knit suspenders and mittens. These were thankless tasks, and she hated them. She did not mind grinding spice in the early mornings or browning coffee and, still wreathed in delightful aroma, preparing salt for the table. It came in coarse rock-salt crystals, but by pounding and sifting she could have snowdrifts to run through her fingers. Her father always noticed when she had done a good job on the salt, and she cherished his rare compliments.

Taking Henry by the hand to drop him off at a small school in the home of a maiden lady who was trying to correct his thickness of speech, Hattie went on down the road to Miss Sarah Pierce's Female Academy. Young ladies of fashion came from as far away as Ohio to attend a school that was known for its social advantages. The Beecher girls had free tuition here since father assisted Miss Pierce with keeping the spirits of youth within proper bounds. Map-drawing, painting, and embroidery were taught as genteel accomplishments, while geography, grammar, and arithmetic presumably improved the minds of girls whose main interest was the opposite sex.

Proximity bred romance, and it was no accident that the

Academy was located next door to Judge Reeve's law
school known as one of the best in the country. Thus,
young men and women of good family had opportunities
to associate with a freedom that was unusual for the
period. What with hay-rides, evening promenades, and
sleighing parties, the older girls kept a romantic schedule
that graduated many of them with high matrimonial hon-
ors.

Few of the students were as young as Hattie Beecher,
and she was fed upon scraps from the educational table
spiced with the lightness and frivolity of her classmates.
But she was a bright little student and often so surprisingly
witty that the older girls made a pet of her. It was a caution the way she could mimic Miss Pierce. Indeed, the
small shy bookworm, in her plain grey linsey-woolsey
among the frills and furbelows of the others, was an uncommon article if one took the trouble to know her.

4

WORLDS OF IMAGINATION

Wʜɪʟᴇ Hᴀᴛᴛɪᴇ might often stand with mind a-tiptoe peering into the keyholes of the adult world far above her, she had a secret realm of her own that no one else could penetrate. Poetic and creative from earliest childhood, she could find playthings and entertainment everywhere. "Pliable as she was to all outward appearances, the child had her own interior world. . . ."

The towering family woodpile was a wonderland as she skipped happily over it on summer afternoons, humming a tune as she looked for the velvety green moss and white lichen trees from which to make fairy landscapes. Bits of glass were the rivers and lakes; cockleburs stuck together were houses; and tea tables of bark were set with the tiniest of teacups made from the backbones of cod. The precious wooden doll was the center of all her arrangements, staring glassy-eyed from beneath its patchwork comforter and holding in stiff wooden hands the blue jay feathers and the berries which a devoted mistress found. Through many

a scrubbing, the doll had lost the curl from her hair, but to
Hattie she was beautiful.

Within the house, Hattie enjoyed the delicious shudders
that came to her when the kitchen chimney crackled and
rumbled. To others, this meant that hams and beef were
being cured there; but to Hattie, opening the door from
the garret and peering within the recess until her eyes
grew red with the smoke, this could be "the scent of brim-
stone" and John Bunyan's own "by-way to Hell."

Her imagination gave full play to all manner of dangers.
Drawn by the lure of the apple bins with their Seek-No-
Furthers and Golden Sweets, she would risk a journey
down into the cavernous cellar that was filled with all possible peril. Sometimes her brothers lurked in the passage-
ways and leaped out with Indian whoops.

And then there were always the rats, a bold robber crew
which long since had staked out squatters' rights to the
parsonage. Defying both traps and generations of cats who
knew when they were outnumbered and outwitted, they
romped all night on the floor of the garret over Hattie's
room, rolling ears of corn which had been spread there to
dry; or they gnawed away at the wainscoting behind her
cot, threatening at any moment to saw through and surround her. When the mighty winter winds swept down
from the hills and roared through the chimneys, rattling
the doors and shaking the old house until every beam
groaned, the squealing of the rats rose higher and higher
until the whole demonic symphony sent Hattie fleeing as
though for her life to the shelter of Catherine's bed.

The parsonage and its surroundings were ever a strong
and silent influence upon the sensitive, emotional child
who was growing up there in her own little sphere of introspection and loneliness, being shaped by them into the

unusual woman she was to become. "There is no independence and pertinacity like that of these seemingly soft, quiet creatures, whom it is so easy to silence, and so difficult to convince."

Matters beyond her ken were forcing her father to spend more and more of his time away upon the roads of his parish, preaching endlessly at prayer meetings to hold the grip of the Puritans throughout his domain. During the year Hattie had spent in Guilford, the people of Connecticut had voted to dethrone the long-established state church which her father upheld. "Down with the tithing man!" the winning majority cried. "Whose business is it to tell me I can't do what I please on the Sabbath?" The common man had broken the rule of the Puritans, whose representatives were no longer protected by the laws and must embark upon an earnest new crusade of powerful persuasion.

In these strenuous days, Lyman Beecher was a hard man to catch by so much as the coattails. Hattie had to content herself with curling up in a chair in the third garret of the parsonage, where her father had his study, and to adore him from afar while he worked on his sermons. High above the noise of the house, this sanctuary commanded a view of ponds and streams girdled with steely-blue groves of pine trees, while within, row upon row from floor to ceiling, were the books that were the intimate friends of her father's.

Hattie had a secure and sheltered feeling to be found nowhere else as she sat there, watching her father writing and turning the pages of heavy volumes like one engaged in some holy mysterious work. It was only in this intimate refuge that she could have her father all to herself, and she would not dream of disturbing him.

Someday she might be able to understand the contents

of all these books ranged about her—like Toplady's *Pre-destination* and Law's *Serious Call*—and then she would have as much in her "cavity of wisdom" as her father. Any book, however old and whatever its title, fascinated her; she was always reviewing the shelves, and one day she was surprised to come upon an addition that was new to her— two volumes of Cotton Mather's *Magnalia*. Like her beloved *Arabian Nights* and a fragment of *Don Quixote*, it was to absorb her for days.

These were amazing stories which the credulous old doctor related: tales of witchcraft; weird reports of voices heard in lonely retreats; accounts of the awful punishments of sinners and the miraculous deliverances of the saintly. To her suggestible mind, every word was as gospel. God had brought a plague upon the Indians to prepare room for the Pilgrim Fathers to settle. "He drave out the heathen and planted them." Cotton Mather was telling her that she, as a girl of New England, belonged to a consecrated race protected by God and chosen by Him for great works on earth. In these formative years, the message struck deep and was planted like a seed in her innermost being.

It was all of a piece with the way she felt the first time she was old enough to understand parts of the Declaration of Independence. For even the most austere of the village folk, the Fourth of July was second only to Thanksgiving; and every child leaped out of bed at dawn to the booming of cannon. Soon wagons were streaming into town from all the country around, and bands of militia that had marched all night were assembling in the village square amidst such a beating of drums and skirling of fifes as to stir all hearts with patriotic fervor. Crowds were pouring into Lyman Beecher's old meetinghouse where strong clear voices were soon ringing out with the mighty Puritan hymn:

> Let children hear the mighty deeds
> Which God perform'd of old,
> Which in our younger years we saw,
> And which our fathers told. . . .

The words swelled and billowed through the house, filling it with an emotion that was heightened by the prayer of Lyman Beecher recounting God's mercies to New England and the United States of America. It was clear indication that the citizens seated here were the vessels chosen to "bear the light of liberty and religion through all the earth" until wars should cease and the whole world rejoice. Lyman Beecher had ever the belief in a millennium, and his children were raised with this "star of hope" shining always before them.

Now Colonel Tallmadge was rising to unfold a long roll of parchment; with head thrown back and with resounding majesty, he began the reading of the Declaration of Independence: "When in the course of human events . . ." While Hattie had but a shadowy idea as to what was meant by some parts of it, she could understand enough of the injustice and oppressions he recounted to be fired with indignation and to respond ardently to the noble sound of "all men are created equal" with the right to "Life, Liberty, and the Pursuit of Happiness." Her country had been founded upon the heroic deeds of men who here pledged "our Lives, our Fortunes, and our sacred Honor" in freedom's cause. To Hattie, these were winged words carrying her on to the heights and giving her visions that would never be lost. She longed to do something, though she knew not what . . . something big and shining bright when she grew up . . . make a declaration of her own.

Her curls were damp beneath her straw bonnet, and her

cheeks were flushed as she twisted her handkerchief, caught by glimpses that were far beyond her age and her sex. What could a mere girl growing up in the early nine- teenth century do to make a declaration, beyond finding a husband and raising a family? If she were a boy, she could put on a uniform and go out and fight, or become a clergy- man. Father intended that all her brothers should become ministers, but she and her sisters awaited no such exalted destiny. The heroic element was strong in Hattie, as it was in all the gifted race of the Beechers; and the gentle child was to be involved in a fateful turn of events that would force her to give it the fullest expression.

With the American Revolution and the War of 1812 behind them, the audience of those peaceful July days in Connecticut was sure that war was a thing of the past for the United States of America. They had returned to the plow and the counting house, certain that bloody trouble would never rise from within the so-called land of the free. They had cut their Old World ties once and forever, amen.

Despite what Lyman Beecher told them about their re- sponsibility to the rest of the world and to mankind, every- body knew that a preacher had highfalutin' notions. Sen- sible men were not about to change their ways. Busybodies among the ladies might start temperance societies, but any hardfisted man knew that a drink or two of rum never hurt anyone. The thing for any man with gumption to do was to mind his own business and to rise in the world, upon the shoulders of his fellows if need be.

It did not at this time occur to them to question the words of the Declaration that "all men are created equal." New Englanders had made fortunes bringing slaves from Africa in sailing vessels, where Negroes were packed so tightly in the holds that they were chambers of horror; the whole of the slave trade reeked with an inhuman stench. And now millions of blacks were toiling upon the southern plantations, being bred and sold like animals with no more rights and no more equality than the beasts of the field. Perhaps it was true, as some said, that the Negroes belonged to an animal race and didn't have souls.

The self-righteous folk of New England were not troubling themselves overmuch about the lot of the slaves; there were comparatively few of them in the North, and according to report, those in the South were better treated and better fed than dozens of white families. Take the washerwoman with the drunken husband and the nine children who lived down the road; kindhearted neighbors were always bringing her potatoes and meat. Charity began at home, and that was the whole of it. Let every man mend his own fences.

Here in Litchfield, after the final flowery oration and the long-rehearsed trills and tremolos of the meetinghouse choir, the crowd poured forth in a holiday mood. Hattie skipped and ran with the other children, all of them wild this one day of the year when stern discipline was laid aside with the workaday chores. The smell of gunpowder filled the air; boys and girls kept time to the beat of the drums as such of the militia as could be recalled from the grogshops marched past in triumphal array. Hattie caught the whiff of camphor from faded Revolutionary War uniforms, recognized the cobbler and the carpenter resplendent in cocked hats and gold epaulets.

The climax of the day was a fight between "the British," "the Indians" in full warpaint, and the American forces; as the flames of a brush fort shot skyward, Hattie cheered. She had known all along that the Americans would win, but it was all so real to her that Catherine scolded her all

the way home. The child would never be able to quiet
down and get to sleep.

With her quivering eagerness, Hattie was always apt to
overdo things, her elders said. She was a hard child on
which to put one's finger; either she was in the midst of
everything, laughing and gay, or she was lost in a world of
her own where she seemed not to hear what anyone said.
She did not stand or sit up straight as a proper girl should;
she was always wriggling in her chair; and neither her
sewing nor her knitting could bear close inspection.
Really, she had no accomplishments!

Even her handwriting was poor, and it was a wonder
that Mr. John P. Brace would even read her compositions.
Miss Pierce's school had grown to such an extent that her
nephew had been added to the staff, and he was asking the
older girls to write each week upon a subject such as "The
Difference between the Natural and the Moral Sublime."
Hattie had heard this discussed at home, and going beyond
her depth and uninvited, she had submitted her first bit of
creative writing. Except for misspellings, Mr. Brace had
pronounced it quite good. He was amused at this per-
formance from a child only nine years of age, and he encouraged her.

Hereafter, Hattie wrote a paper every week because it
was easy for her, and she enjoyed it. While the older girls
toiled and erased and suffered over their compositions, she
had made the discovery that it was as natural for her to
write as it was for a bird to sing.

She had an excellent instructor in Mr. Brace, who stimulated her thoughts and showed her how to express her
feelings (within limits) until, by the age of eleven, she had
reached a dizzy height of achievement. Hers was one of the
three best compositions selected to be read at the annual
school exhibition before "all the literati of Litchfield."

The subject she had chosen to tackle was extraordinary for a girl of her years, but she had tried to develop her arguments skillfully and to answer the question "Can the Immortality of the Soul Be Proved by the Light of Nature?" She was her father's daughter trained by the long series of supper-table debates, but it was one thing to write in privacy and another to have all one's thoughts exposed to the public. She had not even dared to mention her composition at home.

She was tremulous when her father entered and took his place on the podium with other dignitaries to watch the opening number of the program, a biblical drama. As the players strode about the stage in flowing draperies declaiming the lines which Miss Pierce had written, Hattie was afraid her poor little composition would pass by unnoticed amidst such competition.

It was a hard number to follow, and her father was growing restless and bored with the first two compositions. Hers was the third to be read, and as Hattie watched his face with agonized interest, she saw that he brightened. In a whisper that carried clear to the stool where she sat, he asked, "Who wrote that composition?"

"Your daughter, sir," Mr. Brace answered, while her father beamed down at her. She had impressed her father, and she had pleased him. Her pen had won her the first of its triumphs!

5

CATHERINE'S TRAGEDY

The older girls at Miss Pierce's Academy were swooning over Lord Byron now, and the more daring of the law students were trying to imitate the poet who had become the lion of the hour. They affected an air of wild abandon for the evening promenades with the girls up Prospect Hill, hair thrown back, shirts open at the throat, neck scarves flowing. Ah, to forget all for love . . . if not to throw oneself recklessly into passion's arms, at least to beg a kiss.

The staid New England community was being titillated by the romantic adventures of the brilliant young English lord, who was being hailed as second only to Shakespeare, and even Aunt Esther had a volume of his poetry in her prim little sitting room which she permitted Hattie to read. Naturally, the child would not understand these burning flights of fancy, these illicit romances, these outpourings of a tortured soul, but it might keep her busy for one afternoon.

Since Lyman Beecher's second marriage, Aunt Esther spent most of her time in her small house next door to the parsonage, and Hattie was one of her constant visitors. She was a child never done with asking questions or with seeking something new in her aunt's library, which offered far wider scope than her father's. Aunt Esther had a catholic curiosity, and she was informed upon chemistry, philosophy, physiology, literature, and many another subject. The works of the Lord were great, she often said, and "she sought pleasure therein," not shocked by what she might find there.

Hattie was not too young to respond to the volcanic nature of Byron's writing nor to sigh over one who seemed so lonely and lost. What he needed was someone to comfort him. Indeed, like herself, he needed someone to love him. Whatever did he mean by such a phrase as "One I never loved enough to hate"? It was only one of Byron's strong expressions, her aunt said, doubtless wishing she had never exposed her impressionable young niece to one who, as Lyman Beecher agreed, "should have been a noble creature." Instead, he was, as Byron himself had written of one of his heroes:

> . . . an awful chaos—light and darkness
> And wind and dust, and passions and pure thoughts
> Mixed, and contending without end or order.

Yes, Byron was sorely in need of spiritual guidance, Lyman Beecher declared whenever conversation at the supper table between boarders and guests touched upon one whose notorious life could only be hinted at within parsonage walls. The minister's piercing blue eyes searched the table as though he wished that Byron were seated among them. He was wasting his life and misusing his powers; the parson spoke with conviction, sure that if he or some of his colleagues could talk to him, they could get the poet out of his troubles. All that an unbeliever needed was a clear strong argument such as Lyman Beecher could give him. How simple it all was as Hattie's father expressed it: the light would dawn with the day.

Later, when news of Byron's death reached Litchfield, Lyman Beecher sat sorrowing as though one of his own flock had escaped him. Raising his bowed head, he exclaimed, "Oh, I did hope Byron would live to do something for Christ. What a harp he might have swept!"

Hattie also had lost someone who seemed very close to her; and picking up a basket in which to gather wild strawberries, she fled from the house. Byron had gone to eternity, and that could be somewhere outside. Perhaps his soul was sighing in the winds that swept through the trees and rippled the grass, or perhaps it was streaming down at her with the warm rays of the sun. A spirit such as his could never remain in a cold dark grave, but would take wings and soar to the heavens. Throwing herself down into a field of daisies and looking up into the bright blue sky, she hoped with all her heart that Byron was in paradise.

No . . . no . . . it could not be that "the memory of the wicked shall rot," as her father preached in his sermon on the following Sunday. Unconsciously, she was rebelling against her father's harsh judgments, much as her sister Catherine had rebelled two years before when her sweetheart had been drowned in a shipwreck off the rugged Irish coast. As the mournful ballad commemorating the event became popular with her classmates, Hattie had a personal interest:

So now the noble vessel, the *Albion,* she is lost
    Though the tempestuous ocean so oftentimes has crossed;
Our noble captain he is lost, a man, a sailor bold,
    And many a gallant life is lost, and many a heart made cold.

Catherine had been engaged to gifted young Alexander Metcalfe Fisher, at twenty-five professor at Yale; and her father had approved of the match even though Professor Fisher's "spiritual state was not known." He had been a good man in every way, one with brilliant intellect and promise; but Catherine did not know whether he had ever expressed "conviction of salvation." There had been so much else for the lovers to talk about—their hopes and their dreams. The impetuous Catherine had thrown herself headlong into this love affair and, with her sad bereavement, had flung herself at her father in equally tempestuous fashion. He must give her some hope that Alexander's "natural goodness" had saved him. Such a soul could not be doomed to suffer the eternal tortures of hell.

But Lyman Beecher could give her small consolation to relieve her deep anguish. "Natural goodness" was not sufficient, according to Calvinist doctrine. Man was born to depravity; only by rejoicing in his utter damnation could Fisher have hoped to be one of the foreordained few elected to enjoy life eternal. Thus it was written, and thus Lyman Beecher believed.

In Catherine's loss of her fiance, he saw clearly the sign of Providence. In God's design she was not ordained to bear children but to be called to special service. "Doing good" was all that remained to the twenty-two-year old girl—the stern call of duty. It was as though Lyman Beecher had never been young and passionate and devoted. His favorite eldest daughter had turned to him for comfort, and all he had to give her was a stone.

Mutiny raged in Catherine's torn breast, a suppressed undercurrent of anger which the younger children would also experience in the course of their lives. Their father's stern God was intolerable to them; and in their various ways, they would strive to soften Him and add compassion to His works. Caught in the harsh struggle of New Eng-

land theology, but driven by its moral force, they would
work for causes. Henry Ward, later to be the most famous
preacher of his time, would grow up hating the stern religion of his father and later translate it into more popular
terms. Catherine would believe that salvation lay in education. Hattie would write a book that was an outcry against
the sufferings that man could inflict upon man.

Eventually the immediate turbulence subsided, as turbulence will in a close family circle. Catherine would
never be the same again, never the gay and spontaneous
girl who had been the joy of the household; but she was
making the best of her situation by starting a school for
girls in Hartford with the money which her beloved had
bequeathed to her. Her vigorous mind would continue its
development; and the full force of her personality would
be turned upon dreamy, yielding, poetic young Hattie.

But while Hattie could be pressed, she could never be
blindly led. She had her own ways to follow. During the
summer after her upheaval over Lord Byron, a deep truth
dawned upon her. She had been wrestling with the problem of good and evil—as fourteen-year-old girls of a later
age might struggle to find where they fit into life—when
suddenly she found it all very simple. Why had no one
ever told her how easy it was, when her father had been
hammering away at every member of the family for as long
as she could remember?

Walking to church by herself on a dewy fresh morning,
she had tried hard to feel her sins and count them up, but
this had come to nothing. Responding to the birds and
flowers and rippling brooks, experiencing the pure joy of
the universe, she could not think of any sins she had com-
mitted or was about to indulge. Oh, dear, what a mistake
this was on Communion Sunday, when all good confessed
Christians might partake of the bread and the wine.

Fortunately, on this particular day her father had departed from the usual dull didacticism of his sermons to speak as the occasion inspired him. Forgetting all his hairsplitting distinctions, he had spoken of the great love of Jesus, how tender He was, how understanding.

This was something Hattie could understand, and she listened attentively. Jesus was the friend and comforter whom she had always sought; she could love Him with all her heart and her soul. If need be, He could even supply her with a conviction of sin; she could trust Him for the whole of it. She had no further need for worry; Jesus would take care, He really would. He would take care of Hattie Beecher because He loved her; He would give her life beauty and meaning.

Uplifted in spirit, she listened as the voices in the choir went "racing around one after another, each singing a different set of words, till at length, by some inexplicable magic, they all come together again, and sail smoothly out into a rolling sea of harmony."

Such singing was always her favorite part of the church service, and she was to write about it further in *The Mayflower:*

I remember the wonder with which I used to look from side to side when treble, tenor, counter, and bass were thus roaring and foaming, and it verily seemed to me as if the psalm were going to pieces among the breakers, and the delighted astonishment with which I found that each particular verse did emerge whole and uninjured from the storm.

With a tranquility that was uncommon among the Beechers and which Hattie was not long to be permitted to

enjoy undisturbed, she walked home in a state of exalta-
tion. Treading upon rarefied air, she felt one with life's
mysteries; Jesus had taught her. Abstracted all through the
noonday meal, she could scarcely wait to share the news of
her spiritual experience with her father. Hattie Beecher
knew she had had a revelation.

When her father went up to his study in the garret, she
followed like one in a trance and fell into his arms. Looking up at him with wide innocent eyes, she made her
simple statement of faith. "Father, I have given myself to
Jesus, and He has taken me."

For once her father did not sermonize or lecture this
oddly sincere daughter of his but accepted her as a person
with her own intuitions. Since Roxana's death he had been
lonely; and now, deeply emotional and human, he let the
hot tears fall upon his daughter's hand.

"Is it so?" He held Hattie close to him in a rare expression of tenderness and love. "Then has a new flower blos-
somed in the Kingdom this day."

Ecstatic with joy, Hattie tripped away in her high-
waisted Empire frock quite content. Yesterday she had had
much to trouble a girl of her age and her upbringing, but
today she had resolved all of her conflicts. Why could not
Catherine do the same? And William and Edward?

Her father need no longer worry about her, lament as he
had to William:

"While successful in bringing the sons and daughters of
others to Christ, my heart sinks within me at the thought
that every one of my own dear children are without God
in the world and without Christ and without hope. I have
no child prepared to die . . . how can I but weep in secret
places when I realize that their whole eternal existence is
every moment liable to become an existence of unchange-

able sinfulness and woe. . . . Awake to the care of your soul.
. . . A family so numerous as ours is a broad mark for the
arrows of Death. . . ."

Hattie was safe in the arms of Jesus, or so she guilelessly
thought.

6

SCHOOL DAYS IN HARTFORD

One by one the elder children were leaving the parental roof, never to return to it except for visits; and as Hattie came into her adolescent years, she was to join them. With all the comings and goings of this active family and the boarders and guests, her stepmother had long since given up trying to guess how many might appear at the supper table or who might be lodged for the night. She was conscientious, and she did her best; but with two babies of her own now—Isabella and Thomas—she had far more than any woman could be expected to manage.

Sometimes, glancing into her room at night when his father was away on one of his missions, Henry saw her praying beside the bed—praying for her soul and praying also, perhaps, for deliverance from confusion and strain. Though Lyman Beecher was becoming recognized as one of New England's foremost preachers, his income had not increased with his reputation. It was still so meager that it had lost all of its stretch. Thus, when Catherine proposed a slight relief by having Hattie join her at Hartford, Mrs. Beecher was the last one to object. Hattie was growing difficult and ever more moody; she was at the awkward age when she had lost childish charm.

Her sister Mary was already teaching in Catherine's school; and later on Hattie also might prove useful to their dynamic eldest sister. Catherine had rallied from her sweetheart's death with Beecher vigor and—with a resolute dedication that in any less spirited young woman could have been pathetic—had abandoned all thought of romance. Instead Catherine was driving steadily on toward a notable career that would make her a pioneer in women's education.

It would never have occurred to anyone to ask Hattie whether she wanted to leave Litchfield for Hartford. What was decided in family councils was final, and Hattie was accustomed to taking orders from Catherine. No one cared that the thirteen-year-old girl shrank from leaving the haven of the parsonage and the village folk—rough outside like chestnut burs, but often sweet within—whom she was later to put into fiction. Nor could she express to them her love of the beauty of sunset-clad hills and the woods where she had roamed wild and free to gather the first spring hepaticas and violets. She would be back in Litchfield only for vacations, but it was here that she would leave a large part of her heart. Now, at thirteen, she was to be torn up by the roots and tossed into a strange new world.

They had a busy time of it, making over some of her older sisters' dresses and cloaks to fit her petite figure, and sewing plumes and new ribbons on her bonnets to give them a more citified air. Hattie went out to take a look at the pumpkins ripening between the rustling brown stalks of the corn, saw the apples rosy and ready for the annual cutting bee, said good-bye to the cows and horses in the

barn, and bravely clutching a worn traveling bag, turned
her back on all the things that meant home to her.

Feeling like a small country mouse, she watched from
the windows as the stage jolted over the cobblestoned
streets of what seemed to her a very large and bustling city.
Hartford had a population of five or six thousand, and it
had shops that were a marvel to Hattie, accustomed only to
Litchfield's general stores. There were shops overflowing
with silks and satins hard by the jewelers and the silver-
smiths and the hatters, all advertising their wares with
flamboyant signs that swung wildly back and forth amidst
the pelting of the wind and the September cloudburst.

Catherine assured her that she was heading for snug harbor, but Hattie found this hard to believe. She was not
going into the arms of relatives but into the home of strangers; and despite Catherine's cheery reassurance and the
promise that she would see her every day, Hattie had the
forlorn feeling that she was about to be abandoned upon
somebody's doorstep.

By a neat and thrifty bit of exchange, it had been arranged for her to stay with a family called Bull, who in
return were sending one of their daughters to board with
the Beechers and attend Miss Pierce's Academy. It was a
matter of trading one Bull for one Beecher, Hattie
thought, nonetheless a bit cheered by her quip. When her
inner world troubled her, she could sometimes escape from
it into the vein of humor that was a family characteristic.
Earnest and serious, the Beechers could also laugh at themselves.

Catherine barely had time to point out the location of
her school, over a harness store at the sign of the two white
horses, before the stage drew to a stop. Motherly Mrs. Bull
emerged from the waiting crowd to give them warm welcome and take Hattie on to a house that was neat as the

proverbial pin. The smell of stove polish and wax, the brightly scoured pots and pans, the fresh white curtains stiff with starch would have delighted Aunt Esther. Hattie, with her curls in disarray and her cheeks pale with weariness and trepidation, had the feeling that she was the only article in the place that was slightly out of order.

Already she was longing for the airy casual sweep of the parsonage, and she felt awkward at meeting the other members of the family: Mr. Bull who she learned kept a drugstore; miscellaneous boys of various ages; and the oldest daughter who, with long raven locks falling from a comb on top of her head, seemed to Hattie the very epitome of beauty and sophistication.

Mrs. Bull did her best to put her at ease and, leading her to a little room at the top of the stairs, told her that she was to have it all to herself. Her own room! It was practically worth the trip to Hartford to have it! Hattie clapped her hands ecstatically, and her eyes grew blue-violet with happiness. She had never before had her own place to arrange, one where she could shut the door and be private. She could think her own thoughts without interruption here and not have to run off to the garret.

Always she had had to share a room with Henry and Charles, and they were growing into such great boys now that there were times when a girl felt embarrassed. The pretty room was all hers, dainty and feminine and not strewn with slingshots and boys' muddy boots.

Mrs. Bull stood beside her, beaming at Hattie's pleasure, and told her she was to ask for whatever she wanted. She was to feel that this was her home and that Mrs. Bull was her mother. For a girl who had been petted and indulged only at Guilford, this was heart-warming news.

When waves of homesickness swept over her, she could run to Mrs. Bull or to the intimate girl friends she quickly acquired. Back in Litchfield, with her brothers for companions, she had never shared confidences with other girls, but in Hartford many changes took place. At Catherine's request, two of the leading pupils in her school had written to Hattie when she was still back at home; and now both of them were coming more than halfway to keep her from loneliness.

One of them was Catherine Cogswell, daughter of Hartford's leading physician; she was vivacious, charming, and much sought after, but she reserved a little special place for Hattie. The other was Georgianna May, who was to become the closest friend of Hattie's lifetime. Georgianna would share her pleasures, her troubles, and her disappointments through all the years that lay ahead of the two schoolgirls walking along the banks of the Park River in the sparkling October weather. She was to satisfy some of Hattie's deep emotional hunger, the craving that lay always within her. Georgianna seemed to understand, as no other had; and for the first time, Hattie had someone to listen to what her elders called "vaporings."

Georgianna was the daughter of a well-to-do Hartford widow and, as one of a large brood, was old for her age. She was not as lively as Catherine Cogswell, not as popular; and Hattie could have her more to herself. She could always run over to see Georgianna when the Bull household oppressed her. Miss Bull was more interested in beaux and in cultivating her rich soprano voice than in Hattie, and the brothers were always swarming through the house with friends who cast one look at Hattie and decided she had nothing to offer them. She was prim, and she was too young to flirt. Though the oldest son ran a drugstore with a large picture of the Good Samaritan in the window, he had no time to spare for the wayside traveller who sat wistfully beside him at mealtimes.

To please her sister Catherine, who would expect her to excel, Hattie worked hard at her regular subjects and began the study of Latin. She was the only beginner in this ancient language; but she advanced rapidly, trying to catch up with Catherine Cogswell and Georgianna, who were already reading Virgil. By the end of her first year, Hattie was so successful that she had put into metrical verse a translation of Ovid. When she took an interest, she could cram an astonishing amount of learning into a very short time; and once her imagination was captured, she was inclined to put everything else aside and let it take flight.

Now, with a room of her own as an ivory castle, she was further lost in a rainbow mist of romance. Trained by Mr. Brace to write when she had something to say, she was creating a Byronic hero who "sought pleasure with a ravening thirst." Her dream was to be a poet, and she was filling page after page of her notebooks with a play in blank verse, laid in the Roman court of the emperor Nero.

Cleon—for such was the name of the hero and of her play—was a handsome young Greek lord who, after much searching and doubting, would come to "sweep a harp for Christ," as her father had desired from the real Byron.

Painstakingly, Hattie drew a map indicating the situation of the city, the temple of Jupiter, and the sacred olive tree where victors were crowned. The drama opened upon a street of Rome where two noblemen of the court were talking about a banquet which Cleon had given:

LENTULLUS: . . . why, this same Cleon,
He is a perfect prince in entertainments.
Such show of plates and cups both gold and silver,
Such flaming rainbows of colored stones,
Such wine, such music.

The adolescent girl was throwing off Puritan stumbling blocks and restraints as she scratched away with a pen that scarcely could keep up with the images, heady as wine, that poured from her brain. She was always to write with a facility and a spontaneity that allowed her little time for revisions. As in later years, she was too quick and too impatient to go back and make them. As for punctuation, she was to be the despair of her editors. Of correct usage, she was to declare, "I give thanks that I have no responsibility for any of its absurdities." The story was the thing, and now she was swiftly portraying Cleon as a Roman rake among rakes:

> LUCULLUS: We shall live twice as fast while he is here.
>
> LENTULLUS: By Bacchus then we shall be lived to death.
> I'm almost out of breath with living now.

In Cleon's house, "thou'st a fair choice between some thirty couches, Phrygian and Graecian and of every name" where his old teacher Diagoras came to rebuke his profligate ways:

> Oh, then these beds adorned with pearls and gold
> Are made to sit on. Pray you pardon me;
> I am a simple man, used to plain things.
> . . . I hear thou art the common talk for waste,
> And that in riot and loose luxury
> Thou dost outstrip even these degenerate days.
> . . . Is this the Athenian Cleon? Is this he
> Who drank philosophy and worshipped virtue?

Cleon was filling her thoughts when she was awake, rioting through her dreams. In a high pitch of emotion, she wrote with burning intensity:

CLEON: Good master! I am even as you see,
A most degenerate and apostate thing
Convicted utterly. . . .

DIAGORAS: But canst thou tamely sink into a brute?

Shamed, Cleon turned to Christianity, daring the wrath of Nero who "bade the slaves bring in the torture" and ordered his soldiers to lead his former favorite before him. (Shades of the later *Ben-Hur* written by another author.)

NERO: We have forbid and interdict this faith
As what we have good cause to know is ill,
Infecting men with pestilential fumes,
Transforming them to haters of the Gods. . . .

If Cleon will be discreet, Nero will give him a post of honor:

Suppose you be a Christian,
Why need all nature know it; be you quiet,
. . . And worship what you will out of my sight.

But Cleon, weak and pale from the torture, nobly stood his ground and refused:

It is my settled purpose while I live
To leave no word or argument untried
To win all men to reverence Him.

Hattie was far from the schoolgirl who, only a few years before, had written her stiff didactic essays for Mr. Brace. She was writing with remarkable sweep and power, with a feeling for words and the creation of character that was unusual for a girl of her age. Perhaps it was being away

from her father that allowed her to give full rein to the
repressed emotions that now flowed in a torrent with no
care as to where they might lead her. She was writing for
her own pleasure—words that no other eye needed to see or
to censure unless she showed them to Georgianna.

But even Georgianna might be shocked at her lurid
imaginings. How could a parson's daughter know so much
of "riot and loose luxury" and seem to revel in it, depict a
lord sunk in "this luxurious slough"? It really wasn't quite
proper. Hattie was letting herself go; and she was far from
sure that Georgianna, or anyone else, would approve.

No matter, she was enjoying the freedom to do exactly as
she pleased without the restrictions and duties that pressed
upon her at home. Here in Hartford she could write half
the night, for Mrs. Bull did not mind how many candles
she used. Mrs. Bull admired a serious student, and it was a
caution to the good woman to see how that Beecher girl
worked.

Soaring, soaring, soaring through these magic hours of
solitude upon the wings of her own poetry, Hattie was
fighting nothing within herself, as was all too frequently
her habit. She was going joyously air-borne with the currents, released from what a later age would call her inhibitions. And she knew a happiness that she had never
before experienced; she was coming out of the shadows
and flying free in the sunshine.

It was all too good to last, as Hattie must have known.
Perhaps that was why she had been writing so feverishly,
because her time would be short. No young Beecher was
ever long permitted to enjoy such pagan pleasures as
abandonment to the sheer joy of living. Some older Beecher was always standing in the background, insisting that
one must be improving oneself.

In Hattie's present case, it was her sister Catherine, who

came into her room unexpectedly one day and found her scribbling away at her *Cleon*. Overpressed with her duties as head of the school, Catherine had forgotten her own youthful ambition of becoming a poet—as life had forced her to forget other dreams—and she was furious with Hattie for wasting her time on such folderol. Didn't she know that no Beecher could afford an idle pastime? A Beecher must be up and doing—up, up, up. Hattie was almost as bad as her aimless brother Henry, who had always to be driven lest he remain a dunce.

To prove her point, Catherine produced a copy of Butler's *Analogy of Religion, Natural and Revealed* and insisted that Hattie discipline her mind with it. True, the girl had done well in Latin and was being tutored in French and Italian; but Catherine was about to turn her into a teacher, young as she was. There were times when Catherine could be as hard on others as she was on herself.

Hattie hung her head, her brief but halcyon period of self-confidence and happiness in self-expression vanishing. Wistfully she put *Cleon* away to gather dust with the years; but the handsome young wastrel who could have been saved by Christianity—or the love of the right woman—would appear again as the gay and cynical Augustine St. Clare who would thrill a generation of feminine readers in *Uncle Tom's Cabin*.

7

GROWING PAINS

Hattie must love and be loved—this was the dominant force in her warmly emotional nature—and the writing of *Cleon* had been one way of seeking an outlet for the strange deep craving which she herself could scarcely expect to understand. She had always adored her father, and it had never occurred to her not to be devoted to Catherine; but spontaneous undemanding love in return had never been her good fortune. Her brother Henry had felt this same lack; they had clung together like children upon a raft in stormy seas, but here in Hartford she was without him. Thus, her schoolgirl crushes upon Catherine Cogswell and Georgianna were intensified by her need for approval and affection. She was looking forward to seeing them again upon her return from her first summer vacation in Litchfield.

It was during this summer that she experienced her rapturous conversion and felt the love of Jesus surrounding her like the fragrance of the wild roses wafting through the windows of the old meetinghouse. "I have given myself to

Jesus, and He has taken me." Her father had accepted this
statement of salvation, which had come from her soul
without dogma or creed. It had been the sweetest and most
natural of experiences; and it had released her to look up
and not down, forward and not back, out and not in. Left
to herself, she would feel no need to seek further. She
knew . . . she knew that Jesus loved her.

But the conviction had come all too easily to suit her
father, on second thought, or to please Catherine. It was
almost unheard-of for a lamb to come thus to the fold
"without being chased all over the lot by the shepherd";
and they agreed that Hattie required further guidance.
With the autumn, her father insisted that she present herself for admission to the First Congregational Church in
Hartford and have a long talk with the pastor.

Accompanied by Catherine Cogswell and Georgianna,
she went into his study and, simply and modestly, told him
of her recent conversion. He need not worry about her as a
new parishioner since her soul had been saved, she assured
him. But she had come to a pastor who looked with
"melancholy and suspicious eyes on this unusual and
doubtful path to heaven."

She had bypassed the terrible soul struggles which her
sister Catherine and other members of his congregation
were experiencing; and as a bosom friend of her father's,
he felt that she must be forced to be far more serious.
Clearing his throat and looking down at her with awful
solemnity, he asked, "Harriet, do you feel that, if the universe were to be destroyed, you could be happy with God
alone?"

The words fell upon her sensitive ears like the tolling of
a funeral bell announcing the death of everyone—and
everything—that was dear to her. She and God alone—herself desolate? What precisely did the man mean?

She grew pale as the pastor continued his attack. "You realize, I trust, in some measure, the deceitfulness of your heart, do you not?"

"Y-yes, sir," she managed to stammer.

"You know that in punishment for your sins God might be justified in leaving you to make yourself as miserable as you have made yourself sinful?"

"I suppose so. . . . I-I mean, yes, sir."

His piercing eyes seemed to penetrate to the very depths of her soul and see that it was not pure. She was filled with sin, he had said, and she was utterly shaken by the time he dismissed her.

He had cut deep into a highly sensitive nature made the more vulnerable by all the other uncertainties of adolescence. The joy and rapture of that summer morning in Litchfield and the sense of peace which had descended upon her were to be lost for years to come. In their place would come the misery of mental anguish and morbid introspection. The pastor had roughly handled a delicate spirit, and he had done his work well. As he saw the world, happiness and mere natural goodness did not exist.

How foolish Hattie had been to think that she had no sins to repent. That was her trouble: she was always too hasty, too eager. Now, practically as often as she breathed, she could detect a fresh sin appearing to torment her; she was destined for eternal damnation.

This was the somber side of Calvinism which had unbalanced many a mind with the fears it aroused. Like other religious faiths, it was a search for the truth, but the conflict lay in the struggle to give definite answers to the tantalizing mystery of the Unknown and Unknowable. The Puritans had sacrificed greatly to pursue this truth as they saw it. Persecuted in the Old World, they had fled to the New and faced famine, disease, and death for freedom to seek and to find under the eyes of a God of Wrath. The stones of New England were bloodstained, and the atmosphere was gloomy with the conviction that every man was born sinful. Few were elected for salvation.

Questions . . . questions . . . questions. Who am I? What is the meaning of life? What is the nature of the soul? Why must man suffer? Why is there so much cruelty and injustice in the world? These were the queries of man through the ages. Preoccupation with narrow religious beliefs in an earlier America and a broader search leading in a thousand directions in more modern times were alike an expression of man's inner need to grope beyond himself and explore life's mysteries.

Why, when I try so hard, do I always seem to fail? Why am I not happy? How can I tell the difference between God's will and my own? How do I know there is a God when I cannot see Him? Call it religious conflict or psychic confusion—few men in any age could escape it.

As with most adolescents, this was a period of soul-searching for Hattie, a time of wondering and seeking to know what kind of person she was; but it was unhealthily intensified for her by the ominous words of the minister. Now, as she was shortly to write to her brother Edward: "My whole life is one continual struggle. I do nothing right. I yield to temptation as soon as it assails me. My deepest feelings are evanescent. I am beset behind and before, and my sins take away all my happiness. . . ."

With her instinct for self-dramatization, it is possible that she sometimes enjoyed making herself miserable. The thought of the Devil standing constantly behind one could lend zest and pace to the most ordinary events of one's life, as the Puritans had discovered. Religion was the one respectable outlet for passionate natures.

What sins did she have? Once a fourteen-year-old girl

put her mind to it, she could discover scores of them. It was a sin to want the sun to come out when God had willed it to rain. It was a sin to daydream, a sin to desire pretty dresses and jewelry like the other girls and to want to lie late in bed—envy and sloth. It was a sin to want time to herself when pressure was being put upon her to make each minute count. "That which most constantly besets me is pride," she told Edward. "I can trace almost all my sins back to it."

She was rebelling against Catherine, who was making her teach; and this too was a sin. Every evening must be devoted to mastering a new chapter of Butler's *Analogy* in order to keep ahead of a class of students as old as herself. For a girl as timid as Hattie, this in itself was a torture. Often she could not hold the attention of the class or keep her mind from wandering away from the arid subject when, as often happened, she had for competition the beautiful tenor voice of a young man who worked in the harness shop below this second-floor school for young ladies. He would sing:

> "When in cold oblivion's shade,
>   Beauty, wealth and power are laid . . .
> Where immortal spirits reign
>   There shall we all meet again."

Probably it was a sin for Hattie to enjoy such an interruption or to permit her heart to flutter with the rest of the class. With a little imagination, she could picture herself to be the wickedest girl in the room.

Here in Hartford, she had little to take her out of herself as in Litchfield. She had exchanged a robust country life for the cramped quarters of the city, and the healthy romps with her brothers over hill and dale for the nervous and often stifling atmosphere of a girls' school. With long hours devoted to classes and study and almost none to exercise and recreation, she had nothing to dispel the black moods which swept over her.

She was employed constantly from morning until late at night, often with time out only for a bite of dinner. Of her crowded hours, she informed her family that, after spending all day in school, she had to divide her evenings into two kinds of study. During the early hours she read rhetoric and prepared exercises for an additional class she was teaching; then she had to scamper on to the study of French and Italian. It was small wonder that she felt herself to be heavily burdened and that often she was ready to drop from pure nervous exhaustion.

She felt also the weight of her father's fortunes, which were at their lowest financial ebb. Despite her weariness, she knew that she must help Catherine as efficiently as was within her power, so that Catherine could send more money home. Their father's fame had always far exceeded his salary, which never had risen above eight hundred dollars a year, and now it was only in some years that his parishioners met even this paltry figure. Many were slower than ever about paying him cash, and less generous at the annual "wood-spell" which supplied the family with fuel. Far too often they were finding sub-zero weather an excuse for not loading their bobsleds with stovewood and making the long trip to their minister's yard. Hell might freeze over, but they would stay snug at home.

"What did I do at Litchfield but 'boost'?" Lyman Beecher was to remark later on with a note of bitterness in his voice. "They all lay on me, and moved very little except as God and myself moved them. . . ."

As in many another New England congregation, the folk were as tight as the bark on a tree. Some, indeed, were as notorious for thrift as one old doctor who was reputed to have kept all his accounts with the same quill pen for the past thirty years. He had learned how to walk so as to give the least wear to the soles of his shoes and how to place his arm on the table so the elbow of his coat would not rub.

In a community where Yankee economies were stringent, Lyman Beecher was by contrast almost childishly irresponsible in financial matters. He was constantly losing money from his pockets and never checked the size of the bills he dropped in collection plates; but now the facts of life were catching up with him. Though both of his wives had always kept boarders and he had assiduously hoed a huge vegetable garden to supply the family table, he was losing the struggle to support his growing family and educate his sons for the ministry.

He had expected to stay in Litchfield for the rest of his life, but matters had come to such a pass that he could no longer afford to remain. Casting about for a better-paying post, he accepted an offer from Boston to become minister of the Hanover Street Church. At last he was to become "the great gun of Calvinism" levelled against a city that had turned against the old-time religion, and he advanced upon it with fire burning in his veins.

His mind had long been "heating, heating, heating" against what he felt to be the godlessness and worldliness of Boston, and now was his chance to strike. He would be off to convert sinners—not by the handfuls as in Litchfield, but by the hundreds—and turn them away from the theaters, wines, and balls of a city that was "the very seat of Satan."

Catherine was wildly enthusiastic about the Boston move, but Hattie's heart sank. Never to call Litchfield home again? Never to know that the old white parsonage was waiting to welcome her? At fifteen, she felt without shelter against the winds of the world.

8

BOSTON ORDEAL

THE YOUNG girl was as timorous as old Aunt Esther about facing the rigors and complexities of Boston, and it was with reluctance that she joined her father there. After her strenuous months in Hartford, she was pale, tense, and tired that summer, and she longed for the peace of the countryside. She had lost the rosy cheeks and buoyant health that could only be regained by long walks through the daisy fields and on to the streams. She needed to get away from people and be alone where, among the birds and the butterflies, she could take a deep breath and relax.

It was to be quite otherwise in the hot narrow streets of a great and unfamiliar city where her father was already embarked upon a Holy War to the knife. The high-strung girl would have no chance for rest in a household teeming with visitors and questions from morning till night. They came from every class and every circle of society, filling the parlor and filling the air with the excited babble of voices. Lyman Beecher was stirring up a human anthill with his revivals and preachments. "Give up the Sabbath, and the reign of chaos will return," he was thundering from the pulpit where he was unfurling the banners of "Vigorous Action for God."

To a man like Lyman Beecher, everyone who was not with him was dead set against him, and that included the large population of Irish immigrants who were Catholics, plus the Harvard College folk and the hundreds of other freethinkers banded together as the Unitarian movement. The reaction of a whole generation had been so bitter and so strong against the iron grip of the Puritans upon both Church and State that—in Massachusetts as in Connecticut—they had broken these bonds and opened the door to secular power and to theologies other than Calvinism. It was to attack what he termed "the Unitarian devil" and rally the forces of orthodoxy that Lyman Beecher had been summoned to Boston to turn back the clock.

He was at a white heat of enthusiasm, ever reminding the members of his family that the very bones of the Puritans rested within a stone's throw of their door. With a dramatic gesture, he would remind Hattie of her heritage, as he flung his arms in the direction of the old Copp's Hill burying ground. He was a man in his element and at the height of his powers.

Morning prayers had been comparatively tranquil back in Litchfield, but here they left the whole family in a passionate upheaval of emotion. Hattie went on to the breakfast table with her whole body aquiver after seeing her father throw himself on his knees and implore:

"Come, Lord Jesus, here where the bones of the fathers rest, here where the crown has been torn from Thy brow, come and recall Thy wandering children. Behold Thy flock scattered upon these mountains—these sheep, what have

they done? Gather them, gather them, O good Shepherd, for
their feet stumble upon the dark mountains. . . ."

Was Father referring to his own family or was he warm-
ing up for church? Hattie longed to ask him, but she dared
not. Now that she was a bit older, she felt closer to her
father than ever before, but she did not care to confess that
she too was stumbling. With a whole flock of sheep outside
waiting for him, she could not expect him to spend precious minutes with her.

Against the sophisticated horizon of Boston, Lyman
Beecher appeared to many as a quaint eccentric figure
from the past and, with his homespun pronunciations of
"natur" and "creetur," an object for ridicule. His oppo-
nents made the most of the fact that he was launching a
series of lectures on temperance in a church that rented
out its basement for the storage of liquor. And the press
declared that he was an arch-Puritan out to destroy personal liberties and to police everyone's morals; but Lyman
Beecher continued on his evangelical way, ignoring them.
As he was fond of saying, he had once thrown a book at a
skunk, and he was not about to repeat the experience.

With her gift for total recall, Hattie remembered later
how the countless interruptions of the day left him little
time to prepare sermons written in "hieroglyphic notes on
small stubbed bits of paper about as big as the palm of his
hand." He was still working away when the church bells
started to ring for evening services, and her stepmother
sent Hattie running upstairs to summon him lest he be
late. The whole family was on edge before he emerged
from his study with coat and collar awry and rushed down
the stairs like a hurricane.

It was always a major production before Father was got
off to church. Feminine hands adjusted his cravat and

pinned together the bits of paper which he dropped from his hat. Then, with Hattie or her stepmother hooked under his arm like a satchel, he would race through the streets at a pace that destroyed brain and breath. "Then came the process of getting in through crowded aisles wedged up with heads, the bustle, and stir, and hush to look at him, as, with a matter-of-fact, business-like push he elbowed his way through them and up the pulpit stairs."

Hattie had a rare talent for capturing mood and emotion, absorbing them from the atmosphere and later reproducing them with detachment and humor. She was also highly susceptible to the environment in which she found herself; and here in Boston, she was often driven near to distraction. It was as though a tender plant were trying to survive the fiery heat of a furnace.

Her father was overwrought, but he had learned to calm himself after one of his impassioned sermons by using back-yard gymnastic equipment or shovelling a load of sand from side to side of the cellar. Hattie, however, had no such relief. If ever there was a man who believed in the sound mind in the healthy body, it was Lyman Beecher; but he had no such concern for his children's well-being. What he cared about was the state of their souls, regardless of the disturbance his probings might cause when all else was out of balance.

Henry had become so rebellious that he confided to Hattie that he hoped to run away to sea on one of the sailing vessels in Boston harbor and never come back. Father was always so busy talking, Henry said, that he'd never be missed. Hattie pretended to be shocked, but she had an inward turbulence that matched Henry's. Their natures were as volcanic as their father's; and one day they too would erupt.

Some days they were able to escape the tensions of the

household by saying that they were going on a tour of the historic monuments in which Boston abounded, but lack of pocket money seldom permitted them to travel farther than their feet could carry them. For young folk raised in the country, the confinements of the city were hard to endure.

Remaining in Boston, Hattie took to reading everything she could lay hands upon, and sewed and knit with a vigor that astounded her stepmother. At other times she would go "owling about," as her family called it, in a state of abstraction which came over her like a cloud and which they could not penetrate. It was her way of escaping from the turmoil about her; instead of asserting herself, she withdrew. Later on, as a novelist, she would often be living in two worlds, drawing sustenance from the life swirling about her to nourish the characterizations and the images that were to make her famous. She had always been given to these moods which her family thought "odd," but here in Boston they were coming over her with greater frequency.

Sometimes, in her absent-mindedness, she made strange mistakes; and then all the family laughed at her. Recovering herself with a jolt, she laughed at herself along with them, the cheerful and lighthearted side of her nature asserting itself. It was a time of life when other girls her age were beginning to go out to well-chaperoned dancing parties and to the theater, but such worldly amusements were frowned upon in ministerial households. She had few distractions to enable her to see life in a happier light, nothing to stop the merciless process of self-examination and the search for perfection.

With her mind racing, racing, racing ahead of her body and her power to cope with it, she was perilously close to a complete nervous breakdown. It did not help to have her stepmother remind her that she was a strange, inconsistent being; she was painfully aware of it. Like a gangling youth who did not know where to put his hands or his feet, she was nowhere at ease. If she moped, her stepmother scolded. If she tried to appear cheerful all day, her father said her shrill laughter disturbed him.

No one understood her—Hattie's was the plaint of all adolescents. But, unfortunately, no one was concerned about restoring her physical vitality either. She was driving herself upon nervous energy, a habit that was to make her health uncertain for the rest of her life. Now when she said she didn't feel well, they told her she would outgrow it. And they said she was lazy when some mornings she lacked the strength to get out of bed.

They told her she should plan her time better, instead of wasting it; no wonder she complained of always feeling tired. In an effort to comply, she wrote down rules for herself and made a clear-cut plan for her days—but alas for her good resolutions. She found it impossible to follow them with any regularity, and every time she failed she felt worse.

Tossing and turning through many a sleepless night, she wondered whatever would become of her. Writing to her sister Catherine, she cried out hysterically:

> I don't know as I am fit for anything, and I have thought that I could wish to die young, and let the remembrance of me and my faults perish in the grave, rather than live, as I fear I do, a trouble to everyone.

Woe, woe, woe is me! Press a lock of my curls against your breast when I'm gone, and weep with the willow tree. The scene was not an unfamiliar one in the sentimental novels of the period, but it was sadly true that fading away

in the bloom of one's youth was far from confined to fiction. There was a desperate undertone in Hattie's plea
that thoroughly alarmed her practical sister. Father ought
to do something to lift her out of her depression—Father or
Edward.

But Lyman Beecher was part of her trouble; and her
brother Edward, to whom Hattie often turned, had no
time for heart-to-heart talks. After graduating from Andover Theological Seminary, the brilliant young man had
just been called to the great Park Street Church here in
Boston where, like her father, he was embroiled in the
fight to restore the "despised and persecuted form of
faith."

The Beechers were being heard from upon every side.
Catherine's school was prospering so that the proud citizens of Hartford were comparing it with Emma Willard's
famous seminary in Troy, New York. It had already moved
from the quarters over the harness store to the basement of
a church, and now citizens were proposing to take up a
subscription and build her a regular schoolhouse. Catherine was buzzing with her own plans, but she was worried
about Hattie, to whom she had always tried to act like a
mother.

She had no girls her own age to talk with in Boston—no
wonder she had become deeply despondent. Genuinely
fond of her sister, Catherine was ready, as always, to pro-
pose a solution. Hattie must return to Hartford, where she
would have cheerful amusing young society and friends
who sincerely loved her. But first she must have a real
tonic in the form of a visit to Guilford, where their fasci-
nating seagoing uncle had at last decided to throw his an-
chor ashore and get married. Here she could see her beloved grandmother and listen to jovial Samuel Foote spin

his yarns with no talk of sin, wickedness, or predestination. He was practically a heathen!

Soon Hattie was on the road to recovery and was writing to her brother Edward that she was not nearly so unhappy as she had been. Uncle Samuel had pointed out to her that she must try to stop her inward probing and live more externally, and she was trying to catch happiness from the bright surface of things. As she was to write in later years: "those who dive for it [happiness] in the waters of deep feeling" may "bring up pearls and diamonds," but if not "will sink and be lost forever."

From this time forward, her soul-searching was to become milder and less tortured; yet, like the death of her mother, it would leave an indelible imprint. If her mother had lived, she might have been better and happier than she was—the thought would echo through the years for her and for Henry in a wistful refrain. Lacking a mother's love, Hattie had sought to make herself worthy of the love of God, but in vain.

Once Hattie returned to Hartford, Catherine was careful not to overpress her. She had come to realize that this young sister of hers was made of less durable stuff and must be treated with tenderness and sympathy. She need teach only one class, and that in Virgil, which she loved. And she could devote the rest of the time to the study of French and of drawing and painting. Catherine, too, felt the need of exercise, and accordingly she engaged horses so that they could have an early morning canter. As Hattie wrote merrily of herself, she "bobbed up and down like an apple."

Cheeks flushed, curls tossed by the wind, eyes sparkling with pleasure, Hattie was beginning to reveal moments when she was possessed of rare beauty. It was a beauty that came and went like the movement of a flame, when a violet light suffused her large oval eyes and her mouth formed a soft curve from which all weariness and petulance had vanished.

Yet, lovely as she might appear in an occasional side-glance into the mirror, she was painfully lacking in self-confidence, sure that everyone else was seeing only her strong Beecher nose. Little things often upset her for days or for weeks, and she was always wondering what this or that person thought of her. "I wish I could bring myself to be perfectly indifferent to the opinions of others," she wrote to Edward. "I believe there never was a person more dependent upon the good will of others than I am."

One flattered her; another was angry with her; still another was unjust, she thought. She was paying the penalty for her extraordinary sensitivity and desire for self-knowledge. Loving more, she suffered more than those more callous and indifferent. And yet—through this acute awareness of herself and those about her—she was constantly studying character and exploring the deep wells of human nature. Callow though her youthful observations and complaints might seem at times, she was unconsciously sharpening the tools of the novelist.

"I do not mean to live in vain," she exclaimed in an outburst of girlish enthusiasm.

9

FATE TAKES A HAND

Thus far in Hattie's life, her most stirring adventures
had taken place in the rocky terrain of the mind. Here in
Hartford it would be hard to imagine a more sedate and
studious atmosphere than the one in which she now found
herself. The ivory tower of a room of her own at the Bulls
had vanished, and she was sharing quarters with various of
the teachers in Catherine's school. Except for lively Mary
Dutton whom Hattie adored, they were years older and
lived in quiet contrast to the "fiery cauldron" of the Boston parsonage.

Hattie was well-chaperoned; and unlike some of her
friends, she had small chance for romancing. Few beaux
would be so bold as to penetrate a boardinghouse for
spinsters, and Hattie was not a girl who knew how to encourage them. Her opportunities for meeting boys were
slight, and she never knew what to say to them. Probably
she was doomed to languish forever unwed like Catherine
and unlike her sister Mary, who had abandoned teaching

to become the wife of a Hartford lawyer, Thomas Perkins; a career in matrimony was what Hattie herself would prefer.

She sighed over her books on spring nights perfumed with lilacs when young couples strolled beneath her windows. If she had a beau, she might hope that he were sufficiently rich to rent a carriage. She would not care for a tradesman or a carpenter, nor anyone dumpy and fat. What she visualized was a youth who was slim and poetic, burning with thoughts and desires that she could help him express. He must not be so wicked as Byron, but he should have daring and a zest for adventure.

It was at such times as these that Hartford and the Academy seemed unendurably humdrum. Catherine might have a gift for broadening the female mental horizon, but she had no gift for extending it socially. For a school ahead of its time in teaching such solid subjects as Latin, higher mathematics, and logic until it was the equal of many academies for boys and the marvel of Hartford, the goal was to reach the higher pinnacles of learning regardless of how lonely a girl might feel with no beau at her side. Brains were more important than beauty in Catherine's opinion, and she was setting out to prove that a woman's could be as good as a man's. It was preposterous to assume, as many still did, that the female cranium was inferior and less noble than the male. It was still a man's world—and the men intended to keep it so—but education would help women break out of the age-old prison to which custom confined them.

In this mighty pioneer effort to improve the lot of her sex, Catherine had had to sacrifice the softer feminine graces and wiles which, exaggerated among women of the leisure class, made them hothouse blooms given to simpering, swooning, and hysterics.

As for Hattie, she was too poor to dress so as to enhance her charms. Where other girls might be winsome in such confections as openwork cottage hats lined with blue, her bonnets were shabby and plain like her dresses made to fit close to the neck. Other girls might bare their shoulders in frocks of embroidered muslin and silk, but a minister's daughter scarcely dared to reveal so much as an ankle. She had no gossamer shawl to drape with seeming artlessness, no velvet hood lined with fur from which she might peer with snowflake-starred lashes.

However Hattie might long for such luxuries and dislike always to dress in hand-me-downs of sensible cambric and wool, she knew that anything more than the bare necessities was out of the question. Besides, as she had long tried to tell herself, it was a sin to envy those who could afford to buy beautiful things. But wouldn't it be marvelous to have so much money a person could simply let it drip through her fingers?

A girl who dressed like a bluestocking—someone who cared only for books—and furthermore was the daughter of a leading Puritan had two strikes against her. Boys did not take the trouble to penetrate her shy façade and to discover that she had a delightful sense of humor and was neither stiff nor a prig.

Even when she was in Boston, not one of the divinity students constantly running in and out to consult with her father paid any attention to her. She was only someone who came to answer the door; and they brushed past her with barely a greeting, preoccupied with some such serious subject as "absolute verity" as opposed to "total depravity."

Hattie could shine among her intimates, but not in social gatherings. Time and again, where other young women found it easy to draw even divinity students into

animated conversation, she faded away until she was all
but invisible. She lacked the vivacity and the small talk
that kept youths hovering around the others like bees
around clover. It was "little nothings" that made you popular, she observed. Nobody cared that you could scan
Latin verse and teach classes in rhetoric.

At whatever cost, the time had come when the maiden
must leave her meditations and force herself out into the
open to overcome her painful self-consciousness. "This inner world of mine has become worn out and untenable."
But it was far simpler for one of Hattie's nature to make
this discovery than to act upon it. Even in solely female
society, she was still inclined to be too critical of herself
and of others. She was afraid of sounding silly and of making the absent-minded mistakes that were the butt of family jokes. Distrustful of herself, she was also apt to follow
any introduction with the thought: Have they such and
such a character? Have they anything that can be of use or
harm to me?

The consequence was that she concentrated upon a few
friends instead of reaching out to the many, and asked
more of these intimates than they had in their power to
give her. "From past friendships I have expected everything, and must of necessity have been disappointed."

She informed Georgianna May that she was now determined to "cultivate a general spirit of kindliness towards
everybody. Instead of shrinking into a corner to notice
how other people behave, I am holding out my hand to the
right and to the left, and forming casual or incidental ac-
quaintances with all who will be acquainted with me. . . .
From these friendships I expect little; therefore receive
more than I expect. . . . The kind words and looks and
smiles I call forth by looking and smiling are not much by

themselves, but they form a very pretty flower border to the way of life."

She was maturing to the point where she realized that everyone could not possibly love her, nor could she love them—it was in the very nature of things. Most would pass and be forgotten, but not Georgianna May from whom she deplored even temporary separation. Love "is so deeply, sincerely so in me that sometimes it will overflow. Well, there is a heaven—a heaven—a world of love, and love after all is the life-blood, the existence, the all in all of mind."

Why should she wish to love with all love's pains and its penalties? The answer was a simple one; it was the essence of her being to seek love as a thirsty plant needs rain.

Uncle Samuel Foote, with his hearty worldliness and sound common sense, had ever been trying to bring Hattie around to healthier attitudes; and it was he who was a splendid antidote for the dark forebodings of theology which none of the Beechers could escape. Life was to be enjoyed, he told her, describing a sundial which he had seen in Venice. It counted only the unclouded hours, he said, and Hattie resolved to do likewise. She would "let all the others slip out of my memory and reckoning as quickly as possible."

Galloping over the hills in mornings that were fresh with dew and with bird song, she tried to forget the walls of the schoolroom soon to close about her for the rest of the day. Wild and free and giving her steed full rein now that her horsemanship had improved, she could here feel as young as her years. She was never cut out to be a schoolma'am, and she knew it; somehow life would take her away from her teaching desk. Her brother Edward had already left for greener fields in the West, but a petite miss of twenty had no such control over her fate. With her father

as patriarchal head of the Beecher clan and her sister Catherine as chief-of-staff, Hattie was one of its most insignificant members, ever ready to yield to the will of the rest.

Despite the fact that her father still was delivering powerful sermons up in Boston, "each fresh as a bullet from a
mold," affairs were not going well with him there. His
church had gone up in flames, and the wags had been having a field day. When the kegs of liquor stored in the
basement exploded and biblical tracts floated out over the
street, they jeered: "When Beecher's church holds out to
burn, the vilest sinner may return."

Characteristically, Lyman Beecher had a pungent answer for them. "Well, my jug's broke," he said, losing no
time about opening services in temporary quarters until a
new church could be built. However, it was clear even to
Lyman Beecher that the "thunderbolts of God" were reaching fewer and fewer marks here in Boston. To renew their
force he had called in such spellbinding orators as the famous Charles G. Finney, but in vain. Beecher was severely criticized because Finney's revivals had given suggestible folk a case of the fits.

No, the Bostonians were more interested in improving
man's lot upon earth than in preparing for heaven, and
the city seethed with reforms. The wretched condition of
the prisons, the bestial care of the insane, and even the
abolition of slavery were drawing attention away from religious revivals. That angry young man William Lloyd
Garrison was bringing out the first numbers of the antislavery *Liberator,* and Beecher felt him to be a dangerous
radical with fanatical notions.

Though he was never to admit it publicly, Lyman Beecher was too shrewd and too politic not to recognize defeat.
Droves of "the lost sheep" of Boston had no intention
whatever of returning to the fold. He could not, after all,

turn back the clock; the city had outgrown the Puritan tradition. He would never lower the banners of orthodoxy,
but he must carry them elsewhere.

With the opening of the Erie Canal a few years before,
thousands of Yankees from New England were pouring
westward to improve their fortunes along with the "pau-
per populations of Europe"; the West, too, would be lost
to the true faith unless a man like Lyman Beecher had the
courage to follow them. Now fifty-seven years old, he had
the vigor and spirit of a much younger man, and he would
never call quits. Hard, struggling, dedicated years had
built a man whom enthusiasts called a veritable king
among preachers—"the most prominent and powerful in
the nation." It was a reputation that could win financial
backing for whatever new mission he chose, and now the
finger of destiny was pointing to him to head a pioneer
theological seminary that would train ministers to spread
the Puritan gospel throughout the West. Lane Theological
Seminary in Cincinnati, Ohio, would be an outpost against
the Papists and the swarm of other infidels.

Catherine also was enthusiastic about the idea of going
out to a city that was called "capital of the West"; it would
be the very place to start a truly revolutionary venture—a
female college for the training of women as teachers. Great
dreams, but it was not in the Beecher blood to think small,
and father and daughter started upon the long and difficult
trip of preliminary exploration.

With the departure of the dynamic pair, Hattie heaved a
sigh; she had mixed feelings about the whole venture.
Whatever her father and sister decided would determine
her own course, willy-nilly; she had never been permitted
to have a mind of her own. But did she want to go West or
didn't she?

New beginnings, new thoughts, new horizons, new

friends, and possibly romance could await her in the West. Many women were packing up to go out and find husbands; where the most adventurous blood was flowing, the women must follow lest they remain lonely New England spinsters. Yet, as Hattie read and reread the latest ecstatic letter from Catherine, she had her reservations. Catherine was saying of Cincinnati, "I never saw a place so capable of being rendered a paradise . . ."; but Hattie was reluctant to tear up her roots in New England. Where Catherine faced ever forward, her twenty-one-year-old sister looked back.

It was almost beyond belief that the Beecher clan should be about to leave the land of the Puritans where they had lived for many generations. Though Uncle Samuel Foote was already in business out in Cincinnati and waiting to welcome them, Hattie would be moving into a strange land that seemed to her as alien and as far away as the Orient.

Yet little did she know that fate was taking a hand to prepare the shyest of the Beechers for America's Hall of Fame. In Cincinnati, as never in New England, she would be attuned to the pulse of the nation.

As family events and decisions beyond her control were about to sweep her away from the rock-bound and narrow shores of her birthplace, so she would be caught up in the rushing currents flowing ever faster between the free men of the North and the slaveholding South. Living in Cincinnati, across the Ohio River from the plantations of Kentucky, she would see the human drama played before her own eyes and eventually capture it between the covers of a book that would rock the whole nation. The novel would come out of her own experience and observation, her own heart, her own soul.

10

ON TO CINCINNATI

As THE Beecher's plans crystallized, the move to Cincinnati began to assume every aspect of a mighty migration. Catherine's school in Hartford was no problem; the able John P. Brace of Litchfield would come to take charge of it and build his national reputation as a teacher. Hattie looked forward to seeing him once more, though she was afraid she had disappointed him. He had thought she showed real literary promise, and she had practically nothing to prove it. Her *Cleon* manuscript had long since been tucked away in a drawer. She had started to write a school geography at Catherine's insistence; but the rigors of teaching and study had dimmed the flame that still burned bright only in letters.

Soon she was off to Boston to help with the family packing and to hear the last of the fusillades her father was firing from his pulpit, taking accurate aim lest the Bostonians interpret his leave-taking as a retreat. Hattie found her stepmother and Aunt Esther in a twitter of apprehension, sure that they would see Indian savages walking about the streets of Cincinnati as upon the farthest frontier. Though Hattie had her own misgivings and nebulous fears, she was discovering in herself an inner courage and strength that were to serve her well through the years. In order to reassure her elders, she pretended so successfully that this was to be a great adventure that she half began to believe it herself.

She had fancied herself to be a clinging vine, but she could stand up straight and taller than her height when the time came. There would be nine of them in the family party heading West, with four-year-old James clinging to the hand of timorous old Aunt Esther. William, Henry, and Charles would remain in the East for the present; Edward was already out in Illinois; and of Hattie's full brothers, only George would accompany them.

It was fall of 1832 before they were ready to embark upon their long journey with a first major stop in New York. Here, as the family scattered among lodgings in the households of various devout Presbyterians—as was the custom among ministers when they travelled—Hattie followed in the wake of her father. She was bewildered by the maze of streets filled with carriages, carts, and churning masses of folk who seemed to know where they were going and were bent upon pushing there with a jab of umbrellas and elbows. As a newspaper reporter of the time recorded ". . . the streets are so obstructed by the number of buildings going up and pulling down, that they become almost impassable, and a scene of bustle, noise, and confusion prevails that no pen can describe, nor any but an eyewitness imagine."

Lyman Beecher was here—he was there—he was everywhere begging, borrowing, and orating, until Hattie found herself in an astonishing, but agreeable, state of de-

lirium. Her father was raising money for the Lane profes-
sorship in biblical literature, and he had already picked
the man for this post—Calvin Ellis Stowe. At the moment,
this name which was to have such profound significance in
her life meant little to Hattie. She had occasionally
glimpsed stocky, genial-appearing Mr. Stowe at the Boston
parsonage, but she knew only that her father admired him
for his brains.

Though fund-raising had never been a forte of her father's, he was being jubilantly successful at it here in New
York. While the morale of her stepmother and Aunt Esther sank lower and lower, Hattie shared her father's high
spirits. "Father is to perform tonight in the Chatham Theater! 'positively for the *last* time this season'! I don't know,
I'm sure, as we shall ever get [as far West as] to Pitts-
burgh," she wrote gaily to one of her friends.

The New York pace was exhilarating, and she had no
time for daydreaming or doldrums. It was enough to kill
anyone dead, she admitted, but it would not last for long.
Meanwhile, she meant to make the most of these never-to-
be-forgotten days when, like his large audiences, she was
kindled with the zeal of her father's western mission.

When finally they were ready to set sail from New York
for Philadelphia, everyone but Lyman and the indomitable Catherine, now called Kate, were exhausted. To add to
the woes of Mrs. Beecher and Aunt Esther, they were
forced to board the packet without a bit of their baggage.
Apparently the truckman had sent it to the wrong wharf,
and George remained behind to find trace of it. What a
crazy adventure this was; no decent gentlewoman should
ever leave Boston! Not a clean cap or ruffle for a week—the
elder Beechers' world was already coming to an end.

Destitute of fresh clothing as they were, they were received in Philadelphia by rich hospitable folk and by

newspaper notices of such a grandiloquent nature that
Hattie was amused. "This distinguished brother, with his
large family, having torn themselves from the endearing
scenes of their home . . . were going like Jacob etc. . . .
a very scriptural and appropriate flourish." She commented
tartly, "It is too much after the manner of men, or, as Paul
says, speaking 'as a fool.' "

While the Philadelphians were ready to open their
homes, they were not equally generous with their purses,
despite Lyman Beecher's eloquence; and the party was
soon on its way. They overflowed the stagecoach in which
they rode and, led by George, now and again lifted their
voices to sing the stirring old Puritan hymns. George was a
merry fellow, running about to distribute religious tracts
wherever they stopped and, as Hattie said, "peppering the
land with moral influence."

If she were "a-thirst for the waters of quietness," as she
had earlier remarked in one of her letters, she was not
about to partake of them for many a day. She was the
family scribe, keeping a record of their westward trek, and
obviously taking the whole trip in stride. "If today is a fair
specimen of our journey, we shall find a very pleasant,
obliging driver, good roads, good spirits, good dinner, fine
scenery. . . ." Yet as they advanced to the rollicking tune
of *Jubilee,* they were encountering the rough roads and
the jolting that made travel in the 1830's a bone-wearying
hardship. Thirty to fifty miles a day by coach or hired
carriage was the most they could cover before there came a
pause in the day's consternations. "Here we all are—Noah
and his wife and his sons and daughters, with the cattle
and the creeping things, all dropped down here in the
front parlor of this tavern."

They were seeing the majesty of mountain peaks and
skirting the steep precipices of a wild and desolate country

that reminded all of them forcibly that New England was ever farther behind them. They were looking forward to Wheeling and a chance to leave the cramped quarters of the daily coach for the freedom of a "floating palace," as the Ohio River boats were advertised. These boats had the reputation of occasionally blowing up under a full head of steam, but Hattie preferred to think that it was only the Beechers who were about to explode.

After so long and tiring a journey, everyone in the family was nervous and irritable; and Wheeling was to give them slight respite. They were dismayed to hear that Cincinnati was in the grip of a dreadful epidemic, and that it would be unsafe for them to proceed. This was the city that was supposed to be so healthful that people seldom fell sick or died! Now, frightened river travellers were reporting that funeral processions filled the streets under a black pall of smoke from bituminous fires that were believed to stop the spread of Asiatic cholera.

At this news, it was only Lyman Beecher who was not faint of heart. The epidemic would soon abate, he declared; and meanwhile he preached every night while crowds flocked to hear him. It was the will of God that he should stop over in Wheeling to spread the message, he said. No one on earth was quite like her father, Hattie thought. In his strong and determined way, Lyman Beecher was a remarkable and inspiring man with an optimism that nothing could quench. As they took a slower route to Cincinnati and travelled inland by stage, he declared that the bumpy corduroy roads made of logs laid side by side, a misery to the rest of the party, were a positive good; they helped his dyspepsia.

It was mid-November before they reached the smoke-blackened but fast-growing city that was to be Hattie's home for nearly eighteen years. While her stepmother and

Aunt Esther might sniff disdainfully at the smell of the
slaughterhouses and be prepared to find the whole city
uncouth, Cincinnati already had many fine homes and a
real zest for culture. Everything had been settled and staid
back in New England; but here, in this young and vital
city, almost anything could change overnight for the better
or for worse. One could feel it in the air.

While her elders deplored the hogs that roamed the
streets as garbage collectors, Hattie viewed them and other
aspects of Cincinnati with lighthearted girlishness. Writing to her sister Mary, who had stayed on in Hartford with
her lawyer husband, she reported: ". . . speaking of the
temptations of cities, I have much solicitude on Jamie's
account lest he should form improper intimacies, for yesterday or the day before we saw him parading by the house
with his arm over the neck of a great hog, apparently on
the most amiable terms possible; and the other day he
actually got on the back of one, and rode some distance. . . ."

Soon they were encamped for the winter in a house that
fulfilled her stepmother's worst expectations; and Hattie
agreed that it was "the most inconvenient, ill-arranged,
good-for-nothing, and altogether to be execrated affair that
was ever put together." One had actually to don bonnet
and cloak to get out to the kitchen. The whole place was
dark and completely uncomfortable, put up by an old
bachelor who of course "acted up to the light he had,
though he left little enough of it for his tenants."

Hattie was observing and reacting and putting it all
humorously into words, even to a description of the doctor
who attended the illnesses of various members of the family. Frail, feeble health was in fashion among gentlewomen
of the period, and occasionally even Kate permitted herself
to enjoy it. Their doctor was a "tall, rectangular, perpen-

dicular sort of body, as stiff as a poker, and enunciates his prescriptions very much as though he were delivering a discourse on the doctrine of election."

Though she was working hard upon the geography which she had started the previous summer, Hattie had a youthful capacity for enjoying her new experiences in a city beautifully situated between the shining expanse of the Ohio River and the richly wooded hills. But as was usual in the Beecher family, she was not long left to her own devices. Kate was impatient to start her new school with Hattie as chief assistant; and soon she was teaching a class of little girls and admonishing them ". . . about quills and paper on the floor; drinking in the entry (cold water, mind you); giving leave to speak; recess bell, etc."

She was back in the old routine again; and while she deplored it, she knew that it was her duty to bring whatever money she could into the slim family coffers. Still, she yearned for something that would release the real Hattie Beecher lost in "the constant habits of self-government which the rigid forms of our society demand." She felt the need of discovering herself as a human being, not a puppet whose strings were pulled constantly by her father or by Kate. As girls of later years might seek to lead their own lives by going to live in Greenwich Village or the Left Bank of Paris, so Hattie Beecher longed to make a breakthrough.

It was an anguished cry that she uttered to her beloved Georgianna May so far away, but who always understood. Writing to her of Madame de Staël, whose *Life* she had been reading, Hattie admitted that like the Frenchwoman she had vehement feelings made "deep, morbid and impassioned" by the restrictions which had always surrounded her. Her innermost feelings were "repressed, and they burn inward till they burn the very soul, leaving only dust and ashes. It seems to me the intensity with which my mind has thought and felt on every subject presented to it has had this effect. It has withered and exhausted it, and though young, I have no sympathy with the feelings of youth."

She had never been able to dance and be frivolous; such worldly abandon would be unthinkable for a Beecher. Still, even without a Puritanical background, few proper girls of the age in which she lived had freedom to be themselves. The chief difference with Hattie Beecher was that she had the gift of expressing thus vividly the cry of sensitive idealistic youth through the ages:

All that is enthusiastic, all that is impassioned in admiration of nature, of writing, of character, in devotional thought and emotion, or in the emotions of affection I have felt with vehement and absorbing intensity—felt till my mind is exhausted, and seems to be sinking into deadness. Half of my time I am glad to remain in a listless vacancy, to busy myself with trifles, since thought is pain and emotion is pain.

Her pen was burning the paper upon which she wrote, as it would later burn when she wrote *Uncle Tom's Cabin.* Outwardly docile, Hattie Beecher seethed inwardly with rebellion. Though she was seeking to come out of herself in social gatherings, it was an effort that often startled the other members of the company. Seemingly quaint and quiet, she could make comments upon occasion that were so barbed with the sharpness of her observation that they could set the other guests back on their heels. Because of her small stature and her large frank eyes, she appeared to be little more than a child. Yet if ever "still waters ran deep," they did in petite Hattie Beecher.

When the geography on which she had done all the writ-

ing was accepted by a Cincinnati publisher and first advertised with Kate as the author, she did not protest. Kate had
the name and the reputation as an educator, while few had
ever heard of her talented younger sister. Actually, Kate
was claiming only to be coauthor, but she was also cutting
in upon half of the profits. As usual, Hattie remained in
the background while Kate took the center of the stage to
make much of this writing achievement, on which she had
acted merely as an advisor.

In a dynamic family such as the Beechers, Hattie felt
herself to have no personality. Where her voice was soft and
appealing, theirs were argumentative and apt to grow
strident. Her father and Kate were obvious, where she was
subtle and contradictory. She was the sort of person who
was hard to find and to classify.

Was she beautiful? Some who had seen her with her face
all aglow and her eyes alight with interest declared that she
was, and surprisingly so. And then there were the times
when she appeared to be ugly and almost dwarflike, times
when her shoulders slumped and she lapsed into such
vagueness that she all but disappeared. Actually, she was
seldom the same two days running. Even if any of the more
dominant Beechers had ever taken the time and the
trouble to try to catch her in the cup of their hands, she
would have slipped out, like mercury, into a hundred silvery drops. Elusive she might be, but stupid and boring
never.

11

CLOSE TO SLAVERY

As would never have been possible in New England, the sensitive introspective girl was being exposed to many sides of life in Cincinnati. It was a rough river town with its full quota of slick gamblers flashing diamonds, of brawling hoodlums and roustabouts. It was a respectable German settlement where immigrants from the Rhine started vineyards and waltzed in their beer gardens. And it was likewise an outpost of education and culture brought from New England. Almost anything could happen in Cincinnati, and often it did.

Here oddments like the fantastic Bazaar of Mrs. Frances Trollope could spring into being. She was the mother of the later-to-be-famous English novelist Anthony Trollope; and Cincinnati citizens were not soon to forget her scathing comments upon their fair and hopeful city. Mrs. Trollope's western dream having failed her, she had written a book upon the domestic manners of Americans which had been published in the year when the Beechers arrived in

Cincinnati. They could see the weird and castellated building which Mrs. Trollope had erected with the ambitious intention of housing not only a department store and a stock exchange, but also an art gallery, a dance hall, an ice-cream parlor, and a saloon.

Who could imagine such an absurd building back in the conservative East? But who, for that matter, would dream that Kate could so quickly secure financial backing for a school for boys and girls aimed at the training of women as teachers and intended to become a model that would have national scope? Businessmen were eager to contribute; the school would serve as proof that the city had an interest in the higher things of life, despite what that horrid Mrs. Trollope had written about it.

Yet, in the crossroads that was Cincinnati, it was impossible to ignore the specter of slavery which hovered over it like the pall of the recent fires to drive out the cholera. It was one thing to hear about slavery in New England, and quite another to read advertisements and handbills in Cincinnati offering rewards for the return of human fugitives. The wordings were as callous as though cattle or sheep had escaped and were running toward freedom. Hattie shuddered at the thought of the secret traffic across the wide and beautiful Ohio, at the desperation of these black men and women. If any one of them came to the Beecher backdoor, she would do all in her power to help them. . . .

Faced with such anguishing problems as these, about which she could do little, she tried to turn away from them and enjoy her own family's prospects. Her father's new house in Walnut Hills was almost finished, and Lane Seminary was prospering with an enrollment of one hundred students. She was enthusiastic about the Walnut Hills setting. "Every possible variety of hill and slope, and undulations of land set off by velvet richness of turf and broken up by groves and forests of every outline of foliage, make the scene Arcadian." It was two miles from the city itself over a road "as picturesque as you can imagine."

The future of Lane Seminary seemed assured, but Hattie's was doubtful. Again she was sure that she was born to live and die an old maid, not at all like Eliza Tyler Stowe who had become her best friend in Cincinnati. She was the daughter of the president of Dartmouth College and, like Hattie, was timid and petite. Hattie admired the perfection of her delicate prettiness, her fair complexion and auburn hair. They were about the same age, but Eliza was the recent bride of Calvin Stowe who awed all the Beechers with his learning. He could read both German and Hebrew with absolute ease and, since his distinguished graduation from Bowdoin College, had become a leading authority on the Bible.

With no romance for herself upon the immediate horizon, Hattie busied herself with machinations of a literary sort. Her geography had already been so successful that it had gone into several editions, and it gave her courage to enter a story in a competition held by the eminent *Western Monthly Magazine*. When she won the first prize of fifty dollars, all the Beechers sat up and, for once, took special notice of her. This—plus the two hundred dollars she had earned from her geography—made them wonder whether they might have a genius in their midst.

The story she submitted in the contest was called "A New England Sketch," and she originally had written it for one of the gatherings of the Semi-Colons, a social and literary society which she and Kate had recently joined. It was an honor to be asked to become a member and mingle with Cincinnati's leading citizens, but Uncle Samuel Foote had used his influence.

Stimulated by this group to write creatively, Hattie was

at first too shy to use her own name upon her contributions and had hidden behind Kate's. She would shrivel with embarrassment if anyone criticized and knew the work to be hers.

Her initial piece was a letter purporting to be from Dr. Samuel Johnson, and she imitated his style for so long that it was a relief to "come down to the job of common English." Next she had written a satire upon the hackneyed subject of matrimony versus spinster and bachelorhood. Anyone who made a tired old joke about either should be penalized was her humorous suggestion. Her third venture was in the nature of an ingenious hoax; she had smoked a set of letters to make them look old and pretended that they came from a pious country couple.

All these had been mere girlish pranks compared with her "A New England Sketch" where, for the first time, she was daring to make use of her own rare and unusual gifts as a storyteller and show the flame that burned within her. She knew character, and she was writing about something and someone she actually knew—not about ancient Rome as in *Cleon*, not about Dr. Johnson's old England, but about New England and her father. By its very authenticity such a regional study was as new and fresh a departure in American literature as James Fenimore Cooper's narratives of the American, not the European, scene had been. The Semi-Colon Society recognized the significance of Hattie's contribution, and their comments were enthusiastic and excited.

Most of the society's membership came from New England, and they had known such a bumptious young man as the "James Benton" of her story. In real life, he was the young Lyman Beecher who "understood every art and craft of popularity" and "made himself mightily at home in all the chimney corners . . . devouring the old ladies' doughnuts and pumpkin pies . . . and appearing equally to relish everybody and thing that came his way. . . ."

There were few among Hattie's audience for the reading who had not met such a perverse prickly old man as Uncle Tim, penurious in all his dealings with the outside world but generous to his family. Hattie had caught the peculiar tang of New England in the skilful mesh of her words and in the mental pictures she drew, and she was not ashamed to admit to the club that she was the author of the piece. She enjoyed an evening of triumph, and she was at last on her way to recognition as a person in her own right, rather than as a Beecher tag-along.

Moreover, with the extra money from her writing to relieve her always-straitened finances, she was able to indulge in a few of the frivolities and feminine gewgaws her heart had always craved. Though the family exchequer still required most of her earnings, she had a margin with which to buy a beaded reticule and gloves of the softest French kid, and to purchase a length of silk which could be made up with the new leg-of-mutton sleeves. Wearing the frock with many petticoats to cause it to swing out about her ankles and call attention to her slim little waist, she could feel like a young lady of fashion when the Semi-Colons met for their evening soirées. She was participating in a social life such as she never had experienced back in Hartford, and occasionally there was a partner to draw the demure little Puritan out into a gay Virginia reel.

The Semi-Colons were proud of a member who in 1834 had not one but two pieces accepted by the leading magazine of the West. Her second was called "Aunt Mary," and it was based upon her memories of her mother and the family stories about her. Again, she was following sound procedure for any emerging author: ". . . look into your heart and write."

Through admiration of her talent, the editor of the magazine, James Hall, had become a friend eager to see everything that little Miss Beecher was ready to show him. Had she been less modest, this sudden professional interest could have quite turned her head.

To add to her unexpected pleasures during these first years in the West, her beloved Mary Dutton had come out from Hartford to join them as principal of Kate's Western Female Institute so that Kate herself could be freer for the missionary work of opening the whole field of public education to women. What she had in mind was a radical step in a period when most of the village schoolmasters were men. It had been Kate's shrewd observation that men of superior caliber were teaching only as a stopgap until they could answer some "thrilling call to action" as ministers, missionaries, and the like; they were "ready to spring to the first trumpet" that called them. Women must have an opportunity to acquire more than "elegant accomplishments," and to qualify as top-level teachers of both boys and girls since "men of tact, versatility, talent, and piety will not devote their lives to teaching."

With all of these outside interests, Hattie had little time for the morbid introspection which had been so hard for her to escape. Her father's house in Walnut Hills, a two-story brick structure set within a rich grove, was scarcely large enough to contain the life and animation of the large household and the steady stream of divinity students. Besides the nine members of the family, the Beechers had two servants in the kitchen and two in the yard to care for grounds, garden, and stable. Carryall and carriage were constantly on the move to bring provisions and guests from the city.

Anything like stagnation was impossible. In addition to the task of building up the Seminary, Lyman Beecher was

also pastor of the Second Presbyterian Church. As Calvin
Stowe was later to remark of him at this period, Stowe had
never seen a man "wheel a greater number of heavily
laden wheelbarrows all at one and the same time."

For the most part, Hattie found it "an exuberant and
glorious life . . . the atmosphere of the house . . . re-
plete with moral oxygen—full charged with intellectual
electricity . . . nowhere else have we felt anything re-
sembling or equalling it."

Both Kate and her father were dead certain that they
were about to mold the mind of the West; and it was
impossible for Hattie not to share their "vivacity, inspiration, and enthusiasm." With her own literary success to
bolster her confidence and encourage her to write in spare
moments, she was on the *qui vive* from morning until
night, thoughts buzzing in her head like a hummingbird's
wings.

Yet beaux continued to shy away from a young woman
with brains. Mary Dutton, who had always attracted masculine attention back in Hartford, was experiencing a
dearth similar to Hattie's; and this was a slight consolation.

Mary's popularity was confined to the girls at the school;
and when one of them invited her to visit down in Kentucky, she accepted with alacrity. Hattie, too, was eager to
see what lay south of them in slaveholding country, and
together they took a side-wheeler to Maysville during the
summer of 1833. Travelling inland by stage, they reached
the village of Washington, where the student's family was
waiting to entertain them with an openhanded hospitality
and careless generosity that were as much of a revelation to
Hattie—with her background of New England thrift—as
the experience of being waited upon by human beings
who were "property." Like the mahogany furniture and
the silver tureens and the crystal candelabra, the black

men and women were owned by their host and, like any household article, could be sold. The Negroes were well treated here, and they seemed to be happy; but Hattie was disturbed by the thought of their helpless state. Again and again during this visit, she fell into one of her fits of abstraction.

Going to church on Sunday, she saw an exotic haunting type of beauty among several of the women who sat in rear pews. They were women with ivory skins who moved with a sinuous grace, women with dark thick-lashed eyes in which Hattie caught an expression of infinite sadness. They were quadroons, her hostess informed her, reviewing the masters to whom they belonged. "Mixed blood, you know," her hostess whispered as they drove away in the carriage which had brought them to church.

Yes, Hattie did know. One of the family tragedies had been that of her mother's sister, Aunt Mary Hubbard, who had married a West Indian planter only to discover that he had a Negro mistress and a whole family of sons and daughters half-white. Aunt Mary had seen how powerless slaves could be to defend themselves against the lust of their masters; as a bride, she had fled back to her New England home with the cry, "Oh, that this island would sink beneath its load of shame and misery!"

Beyond her absent-mindedness and the amusing incidents she collected to entertain her family, Hattie gave little evidence of her profound reaction to these summer days in Kentucky. She had had a glimpse of plantation life when they were entertained at one of the big white-pillared houses in the midst of the slave cabins. Though chubby pickaninnies laughed in the arms of their mothers, she could picture it otherwise. Her imagination supplied tear-drenched scenes of separation when husband, wife, and child might be sold away from each other, never to meet again in this life. She knew that she was seeing the system of slavery in its mildest form here in Kentucky; but she was sure that wherever human beings had no control over their destinies, there could be no "best." In Kentucky:

> The general prevalence of agricultural pursuits of a quiet and gradual nature, not requiring those periodic seasons of hurry and pressure that are called for in the business of more southern districts, makes the task of the Negro a more healthful and reasonable one; while the master, content with a more gradual style of acquisition, has not those temptations to hard-heartedness which always overcome frail human nature. . . .

This observation and the scenes which she witnessed on this summer visit would remain at the back of her mind for eighteen years before she brought them out again with her marvelous facility for total recall. She had glimpsed "Eliza" in one of the lovely quadroons; she had seen the plantation of "Colonel Shelby"; and she had not forgotten the slave cabin in which she was to place Aunt Chloe and Uncle Tom. It was "a small log building close adjoining to 'the house.' In front it had a neat garden patch where strawberries, raspberries, and a variety of fruits and vegetables flourished under careful tending."

For all her friend Mary Dutton knew, Hattie "did not seem to notice anything in particular that happened, but sat much of the time as though abstracted in thought. When the Negroes did funny things and cut up capers, she did not pay the slightest attention to them. Afterwards, however, in reading *Uncle Tom's Cabin,* I recognized scene after scene of that visit portrayed with the most minute fidelity. . . ."

It would take years and a succession of other vivid real-life experiences before the whole panorama unfolded and the story took form—years before the great stage was set and the actors emerged upon cue. Meanwhile, in the small theater of her own life, events were moving faster for Hattie Beecher than she might have dreamed.

12

A SYMPATHETIC EAR

THEY HAD lived less than two years in Cincinnati when the restless active Beechers were again on the road. Lyman Beecher was going East in the summer of 1834 on a money-raising tour, turning his back upon what was to be a crisis in his western affairs. Kate was travelling as an inspired missionary in the cause of better and higher education for women, and Hattie was heading for Massachusetts and Henry Ward's graduation from Amherst.

Hattie's journey would take her by stage to Toledo, and thence by Lake Erie steamboat to Buffalo; but by now she felt herself to be an experienced traveller. She and Mary Dutton were going together, and in other years she would have shied away from making the long journey in the sole company of another young woman. These days, however, she had a new lift to her slight shoulders and a new bright-ness in her eyes that came from a degree of independence which her writing afforded her. She was no longer living off the scraps from the Beecher table; she had a little money of her own to spend. Kate had never paid her a regular salary, but now there was money in the till upon which she could modestly draw.

As she and Mary settled themselves in the close quarters of the Ohio stagecoach, she amused herself by making a study of her fellow passengers. Like an artist with his pencil, she often seized an opportunity to make portraits with quick, telling strokes. There was a New Orleans girl "looking like distraction, as far as dress is concerned, but with the prettiest language and the softest intonations imaginable, and one of those faces which, while you say it isn't handsome, keeps you looking all the time to see what it is that can be so pretty about it."

And then there was the woman who fussed and fidgeted all through the day's ride, a perpetual motion type, in contrast with a man who seemed "the most gentlemanly, obliging man that ever changed his seat forty times a day to please a lady. Oh, yes, he could ride outside—or, oh certainly, he could ride inside—he had no objections to this, that, or the other. . . ."

But it was when they reached Niagara Falls that the young woman of barely twenty-three rose to an as yet unfathomed height of power that was to mark the finest of her later work. Uninhibited as to words or emotions, she responded with the very fiber of her being:

Let me tell, if I can, what is unutterable. I did not once think whether it was high or low; whether it roared or didn't roar; whether it equaled my expectations or not. My mind whirled off, it seemed to me, in a new strange world. It seemed unearthly, like the strange, dim images in the Revelation.

I thought of the great white throne; the rainbow around it; the throne in sight like unto an emerald; and oh! that beau-

tiful water rising like moonlight, falling as the soul sinks
when it dies, to rise refined, spiritualized, and pure; that
rainbow, breaking out, trembling, fading, and again coming
like a beautiful spirit walking the waters.

Oh, it is lovelier than it is great; it is like the Mind that
made it: great, but so veiled in beauty that we gaze without
terror. I felt as if I could have *gone over;* it would be so
beautiful a death; there would be no fear in it. I felt the
rock tremble under me with a sort of joy. I was so maddened
that I could have gone over too, if it had gone. . . .

No pagan could have been more enraptured. The little
Puritan burned with an ardor of spirit that could never be
contained within the narrow walls of Calvinism. Without
regard to scripture or dogma, she felt capable of throwing
herself upon an altar of love for the whole universe.

From Niagara Falls she travelled on by stagecoach towards the New England which was so familiar to her that
she rejoiced in every stone of the neatly piled fences. This
was her true home as opposed to the sprawling unconven-
tional West; here was the precision and order of Yankee
tradition and custom. It was good to see Henry and to note
how popular her favorite brother had become with his
classmates and how well he had done in his studies. Also,
he had overcome the thickness of tongue which, like his
slowness at books, had plagued him since childhood.
Henry Ward was beginning to find himself—she could
sense it—and he was showing promise of his future as a
famous pulpit orator.

With all their old-time camaraderie re-established,
Henry whisked her away to visit old friends and relatives,
to sit beside welcoming hearths and to bubble as gaily as
teakettles. Hattie was always to feel somewhat of an exile
out in Cincinnati, but having Henry with her this time

would be a great help. She need not feel wistful at leaving him behind, for he was joining the family there.

It was foolish for Hattie to pine for what was presently impossible—a home in New England. She needed to remind herself that Cincinnati was not actually at the end of the world, and with the present astonishing speed of their travel, she could readily come back East for visits. Marvelous to relate, she and Henry were able to make the journey by mail-coach in the mere space of ten days.

Yet a sad vacancy awaited her in Cincinnati; her bosom friend Eliza Tyler Stowe was dead. Wilting with the late summer heat during another cholera siege, Eliza was gone like some exquisite flower. When Hattie loved, she gave her whole heart; and she had sincerely loved Eliza Tyler Stowe.

As for Calvin Stowe, he was all but inconsolable in his sudden bereavement. Theirs had seemed to Hattie to be the perfect marriage; it had been one of mutual adoration. Observing them together, Hattie had often wondered whether similar good fortune could ever be her lot.

Calvin Stowe was a strange man and one who was hard to get to know, but that was small wonder when he had such a brain. Eliza had confided to Hattie that he always slept with a copy of the *Divina Commedia* and the Greek Testament under his pillow and could read them both in their original tongues as readily as anyone else might peruse the columns of a newspaper. His knowledge of Greek and Hebrew, German and Italian was a big talking point in the curriculum offered to the students at Lane, among whom he was extremely popular.

He could tell amusing anecdotes of his New England boyhood, and he had a rare ear for dialect, as Hattie had observed at social gatherings; but also he was reputed to have visions and visitations from the world of the spirit.

He kept a harp in the corner of his bedroom, and now he claimed that Eliza appeared to him frequently and struck it with thin ghostly hands. At this report, sympathetic folk agreed that the star member of the Lane faculty must be almost beside himself with grief.

The Seminary, too, was in a state of dire consternation, but Hattie was sure that her father could set all to rights. Overcome by his sorrow, Calvin Stowe had not been able to cope with an open insurrection among the students which had started shortly after Beecher's departure. It stemmed from the still-infant cause of abolition, which had entered the school during the previous year with the person of the able but fanatical Theodore Weld. The young man had enrolled in Lane with a large company of followers; and he had organized a vociferous company to demand immediate freedom for the slaves. The Lane Anti-Slavery Society had taken advantage of Beecher's absence in the East to court the favor of the thousand free Negroes residing in Cincinnati, thereby openly flying in the face of public opinion.

Cincinnati was peculiarly sensitive to such flagrant agitation as Weld's because much of its prosperity depended upon friendly river trade with the South; pocketbooks would suffer should irresponsible radicalism spread through the city unchecked. Had they a serpent in their midst in the shape of this new seminary? The newspapers raised a furious outcry.

Lane was positively dedicated only to the cause of education and religion, the trustees reassured them, hastily voting not only to abolish the Anti-Slavery Society but to prohibit all discussion of slavery in any room of the school. Lyman Beecher might have handled the matter more diplomatically; but, before he could hurry back from the East, Weld had marched out of the Seminary in a rage followed by over half of the students. Further, the news spread nationwide that Lane was reactionary and intolerant. Folk leaped to the conclusion that it had taken a stand, not only in support of slavery, but in opposition to all freedom of speech.

The truth of the matter was that Lane, as a fledgling institution hoping to become the great theological school of the West, felt it could not afford to be sidetracked by becoming identified with the slavery issue which was only then beginning to appear in the North. Hotheads were rushing in where wiser men must hesitate.

Some might view it as an irremediable evil and a sin that could not be eradicated, one beyond human power to correct. Others, like Lyman Beecher and Calvin Stowe, felt that gradual emancipation by orderly process of law and colonization in Africa must be the eventual solution. The vast majority, however, still preferred to shut their eyes to the whole intricate problem.

Lyman Beecher was a crusader, but he was not about to ride the wild horses of abolition being whipped up by Theodore Weld. He had always agreed that slavery was a moral evil, but he had regard for property rights and the knowledge that no such vast abuse as slavery could be corrected overnight by impassioned idealists.

Could it be possible that such an upstart as Weld might defeat Beecher's mighty purpose of bringing to the West the religion of the Puritans? Lyman Beecher pooh-poohed the notion as preposterous. He had been eminently successful in his money-raising campaign through the East, and he was sure that the whole trouble would blow over as an outburst from hot-blooded youth.

Looking at his half-deserted classrooms that fall, he was optimistic that they soon would fill up again with future preachers for Ohio, Indiana, and Illinois. He was nearing sixty, but his energy and his drive were those of a man half his age. He never remained long submerged in the spells of "hypo" and depression which sometimes assailed him. Now his immediate job was to rally the spirits of the faculty—especially those of Calvin Stowe—and to answer anxious queries from the East about the whole Weld affair. One of the school's major endowments came from a man who had recently embraced the abolition cause, and it was important for Lyman Beecher to perform to the hilt as an astute politician.

In the scant free time left over from her teaching, Hattie also was trying to console the widower. Having been so close to Eliza, she lost the reserve that kept her from talking freely to a man who was not a member of her family; she spent hours with Calvin extolling the virtues of the cherished person they had lost. Eliza would wish her to see that Calvin was not lonely and that he was supplied with the little comforts and the understanding that only a sympathetic woman could give him.

Small of stature like Eliza, soft-voiced, and moving about his bachelor quarters to straighten up his study and wash the dishes untidily piled up in the sink, Hattie came and went with increasing frequency. This careless, rumpled man nine years her senior was childlike in his helplessness, and he needed someone to take care of him.

Meanwhile, that fall she and her father made a trip along the Ohio River that was to have deep significance. They were attending a meeting of the Presbyterian Synod in the little town of Ripley and were the guests of the local clergyman and his pleasant, bustling wife. Their modest house on a high bluff commanded an enthralling view of the river and of the blue hills across its wide expanse that marked the shores of Kentucky.

Calvin Stowe joined the Beechers under the same roof;

and each night, as it grew dark and the lamps and candles were lit, their host placed a lantern in precisely the same position on a table in one of the windows which overlooked the river. Hattie observed that this light could not be seen from the town which nestled beneath the bluff, nor from the road, and she was curious about it.

What could be out there in the blackness of the night where one could see only the twinkle of the stars and occasionally the festive salons of passing riverboats? Did the lantern have a secret meaning; was it some kind of signal?

When she and the others could no longer contain their curiosity and questioned the Reverend Rankin, he seemed perturbed, as he scrutinized the faces surrounding him. Hattie demure with her ringlets, the famous pastor Lyman Beecher, with his strong chin and flashing eyes, sitting between her and genial, balding Calvin Stowe. It was as though he wondered whether he could trust them. He was aware of the recent unpleasantness at Lane and of the accusations that it was proslavery, but he decided to take the chance. Recent years had made him a canny judge of faces.

In a low voice, Rankin revealed that this house of his was a station on the secret route that led escaping slaves to freedom. The light in the window was a beacon to guide desperate human beings to a friend who would not betray them. They would find food and shelter here, and a guide to the next haven upon the long and perilous journey that, God willing, would take them on to safety in Canada.

Quiet resistance was what Rankin offered, in contrast to the obstreperous outcries of the abolitionists. Calm courage . . . it took a brave man to face the heavy penalties should his activities be discovered. Hattie had heard about the "underground," but she had thought that only Quakers had this daring and this dedication.

Long after her own lamp was blown out for the night,

she lay in her bed unable to sleep, listening for sounds about the corners of the house, wondering what the flickering shadows outside around the stable might conceal. With all her heart and soul, she too longed to be of some assistance to these souls held in bondage, these millions of blacks that stretched like a sad and sighing sea across the South.

She could not shut from her eyes the vivid picture she had painted for herself when Reverend Rankin told them about one of his most dramatic experiences. It was beyond belief, but it had actually happened. One bitter March night he had opened his door to a young Negro woman who, clutching her baby in a hard-frozen blanket, had fallen at his feet. Revived by his wife with hot food and drink, she was able to tell him her story.

She had been so desperate and so driven when she heard that her child was to be sold away from her that she had fled with him across the rotten spring ice of the Ohio River. Somehow it had held under her as she leaped from block to block, and now she was at Rankin's mercy with bloody, beaten feet. No human could have made it across the Ohio with the ice cracking and swaying under her; but somehow, by some miracle, she had. Rankin had spirited her away upon a midnight journey in the hooded carriage which he kept for such purposes, and when he returned he had heard the mighty boom of the ice. Spring and the season of open water had set in. . . .

"Eliza crossing the ice." Hattie could not know then that the tale which the good Reverend had unfolded to them would become part of her phenomenal first novel, and that it would make millions weep:

In that dizzy moment her feet scarce seemed to touch the ground, and a moment brought her to the water's edge. Right on behind they came; and, nerved with strength such as God gives only to the desperate, with one wild cry and flying leap, she vaulted sheer over the turbid current by the shore, on to the raft of ice beyond. It was a desperate leap—impossible to anything but madness and despair. . . .

Hattie's pillow was wet with the tears she was shedding over the Reverend's tale; but as she tossed and turned, she liked to remember that Calvin Stowe had been equally moved by it. She could not possibly care for any man who did not respond with all his being to this human appeal.

13

RICH ONLY IN LEARNING

Wɪᴛʜ ʜᴇʀ beloved friend Eliza so recently dead, Hattie did not care to admit that she was looking forward to the hours she could spend with Calvin Ellis Stowe. It was a new experience for her to feel needed; this was why she was seeing more and more of him, she tried to tell herself. Seeing him in a romantic light so soon after his wife's death would be highly improper.

Nevertheless, she found herself to be increasingly absorbed in the welfare of this scholarly man with the droll wit who showed such interesting contradictions of character. If she herself had sometimes been thought odd in her behavior, Calvin Stowe was twice as strange. They were both of them unusual, not run of the mill; but Hattie had never abandoned reality to live entirely in a world of visions, as Calvin declared that he had.

Mystic experiences were not uncommon in the world of her time—hallucinations, delusions, trances, prophesies. In the misty hills of upstate New York, Joseph Smith had found golden tablets engraved with ancient writings and the miraculous spectacles with which to decipher them; and he had recently set forth as the messiah of a new order called Mormonism.

That which one sees is not made of that which does appear; illusions are more real than things. Many in New England were being swept into various interpretations of transcendentalism; and Hattie herself had glimpsed psychic meanings in her periods of "owling about." Yet it was an uncanny experience to hear a stout logician like Calvin Stowe, who declared he had no imagination whatever, stand up and read his paper before the Semi-Colon Club one evening.

Blunt and tactless, he was also so honest that he could not have been inventing this account for the sole purpose of titillating his audience. As early in his childhood as he could remember, he said, he had seen a multitude of objects in a state of great animation passing through floors and walls, and sometimes assuming menacing forms. A psychologist might be able to explain this phenomenon, he declared, continuing his report with scientific detachment. Almost nightly during his childhood he had known the consoling presence of a cheerful phantom called Harvey, but once he had awakened to discover a full-sized skeleton lying next to him in the bed.

Because Calvin Stowe had been a poverty-stricken, lonely child brought up in Natick, Massachusetts by a widowed mother and maiden aunts, the psychiatrists of a later day might have discerned that these day-and-night phantoms were a small boy's way of escape from the insecurity and anxiety that surrounded him. Sometimes he had been terrified by bands of little devils, and sometimes made gay by dancing fairy troops. And it was not until he was a half-grown lad that he realized that others did not have these unearthly visitations. Calvin Stowe also confessed to his audience that he had had a morbid love for his friends that "would almost burn up his soul."

Hattie Beecher herself could have written that line. Calvin's sorrow over Eliza had led her to believe that, beneath his rotund exterior, the man had a richly emotional nature; and his paper was further revelation of it. He was no dry-as-dust scholar, she thought, but a man who could throb with his passions.

While his prolonged melancholy following Eliza's death seemed morbid to others, she could excuse it. Unfortunately, she was not aware that he was highly unstable and that his spells of melancholy and hypochondria were habitual.

She was further impressed with Calvin Stowe when that winter he delivered a series of sermons that displayed his phenomenal knowledge of the origins of the books of the Bible. He was an excellent speaker with a power of delivery that rivalled her father's, but what she did not realize was that he lacked her father's indomitable courage. "If ever a woman feels proud of her lover, it is when she sees him as a successful public speaker," she was to write later in one of her novels, *Dred*.

Seeing Calvin Stowe on the platform was a significant turning point in the tide of her feelings. The two were drawn together further by their mutual loyalty to Lyman Beecher, who, in addition to his troubles at the Seminary, was being attacked in his pulpit with heresy charges made by the Rev. Dr. Joshua Wilson, who had ever been jealous of Beecher's prestige. Beecher successfully defended himself, but the sting would remain.

Hattie's regard for Calvin Stowe was moving from compassion into far deeper channels. Was it romantic love that

she felt for him? She was weary of being alone, and she
needed a man upon whose broad shoulders she could lean
and upon whom she could pour all the love and tenderness
so long stored up in her heart. Calvin Stowe, in turn, required a woman who could give him her rare understanding.

Everyone said that Calvin Stowe had an important career ahead of him; and while Hattie was not mercenary
nor overly ambitious, it would be a relief to have hope of
rescue from poverty's brink. To be sure, Stowe's salary had
been cut by the present small student enrollment, but her
father was always assuring him that Lane Seminary would
soon be back on its feet.

Hattie had her practical side, but soon she was lost in
roseate dreams of the future. She was not so blind as to
consider Calvin Stowe handsome, nor did he wear his melancholy with the jaunty air of the poet who had occupied
the dreams of her girlhood; but—and facts were facts—she
was no longer a girl.

Hattie had reached the age of twenty-four, and according
to the views of her time, she was approaching the deadly
mark of spinsterhood. Kate was strong and militant, and
she could face life unwed. Moreover, unlike her sister,
Kate had a lost lover for whom to mourn, whereas Hattie
had not so much as a pressed rose or a stolen kiss among
her book of memories. She had been too withdrawn and
too timid to collect sentimental souvenirs, and she had no
romantic escapades to confess when Calvin asked her to
marry him.

The announcement came as no surprise to their Cincinnati intimates, who had for some time been in expecta-
tion of it. After a short engagement, she was uttering the
last cry of her maidenhood to Georgianna May on January
6, 1836. Only a few moments before the simple ceremony,

she was seated at her writing desk, gripping the pen which Calvin Stowe was to snatch out of her hand:

> Well, my dear G., about half an hour more and your old friend, companion, schoolmate, sister, etc. will cease to be Hattie Beecher and change to nobody knows who. My dear, you are engaged and pledged in a year or two to encounter a similar fate, and do you wish to know how you shall feel? Well, my dear, I have been dreading and dreading the time, and lying awake all last week wondering how I should live through this overwhelming crisis, and lo! it has come and I feel *nothing at all.*

The letter trailed off, not to be finished until several weeks later, as Hattie rose to stand beside Calvin Stowe while the family circle closed about them. Among those absent was her stepmother who had died during the previous summer, shortly before the gathering of the entire Beecher clan in Cincinnati for a family reunion. There had been eleven children, with the white-haired patriarchal father of them all completing the full Beecher's dozen.

Tiny and slim in her high-waisted gown with the puffed leg-of-mutton sleeves, Hattie made her vows in a low voice that trembled with emotion, but the luminous eyes that met Calvin's when he kissed her were violet-blue with happiness. A thrill swept over her as his strong hand gripped her fingers as though he would never release them. Gone were the years of lonely striving and brooding, she thought; she would have Calvin always beside her.

Yes, she would try to be the perfect wife, even the perfect housekeeper, and, when the time came, the perfect mother—this she had determined in the last days of her maidenhood. But first of all they would be lovers, she and

Calvin. She longed to have him take her into his arms; and yet she lingered within the familiar circle of her family, looking across at Calvin as though he had become almost a stranger, an intruder upon her shyness and modesty, her old established ways.

When the door of the home which Calvin had shared with Eliza closed shut upon them, she wondered what a newly married pair might talk about, but Calvin sealed her lips.

And now, my dear, perhaps the wonder to you, as to me is how this momentous crisis in the life of such a wisp of nerve as myself has been transacted so quietly. My dear, it is a wonder to myself. I am tranquil, quiet, and happy. . . .

Thus she resumed her letter to Georgianna when she returned from her wedding trip. Two days after their marriage, they took the coach for Columbus, skidding over the icy roads of January to combine business with honeymoon. Any bride not raised in a minister's household might have resented professional intrusion upon private bliss, but Hattie was proud that the man she called husband had been asked to address the Western College of Teachers on education in Prussia. Calvin Stowe's knowledge seemed to be as unlimited as her confidence in him.

Once back in Walnut Hills, she mingled her few possessions with those left by the beloved Eliza and directed her full attention toward housekeeping with a stock of china for parlor and kitchen that had cost eleven dollars. It had been her sole wedding present where, years later, her daughter Georgie would receive gifts amounting to over twenty-five thousand. No matter, Hattie was used to making little do the work of much. What did lack of money matter when one was content? Calvin was rich in learning, but his worldly goods consisted almost entirely of a store of books piled from the floor to the ceiling of his study.

As Hattie busied herself about the kitchen scrubbing the floor to whiteness and making pots and pans gleam, she was glorying in a home of her own. Calvin's income would soon improve, she was sure, and meanwhile she could braid rugs from scraps of old coats and dresses, and find bargains from which to crisply curtain the windows.

Calvin seldom noticed housekeeping details so long as she kept his newspaper neatly folded and did not leave it spread about like the "guts of a goose," as he crossly re-marked. She tried to have the fire glowing for him when he returned from his classrooms and, soothing his crotch-ets, settled down beside him "domestic as any pair of tame fowl you ever saw."

He was the lord of the household, and she the hand-maiden who wished to serve his every desire. Though Cal-vin was clumsy about repairing smoky flues or thawing out the water pump when it froze, she was discovering how to meet household emergencies without troubling her hus-band about them. When he complained of minor ailments, she concocted home remedies and tried to lift up his spir-its. It was a wife's duty to encourage her husband and keep him in good health, she thought, keeping to herself the misgivings that assailed her even during these first months of marriage. It was a period of adjustment, she knew, but where was the sturdy oak on which she had counted?

Was she failing Calvin as Eliza had not? Or had Eliza, too, seen him sunk in these spells of depression and self-pity that must run their course? Hattie put aside her own moods to cheer him; perhaps this was all a part of getting used to a husband who could rise from his sickbed when company came and entertain them with the humor that could make him the most engaging of companions. He had a winning personality, when he chose, and children adored him.

He would make an admirable father for the child she expected. The happy news was confirmed only a few days before a trip to Europe loomed in the offing. The state legislature had voted funds to send Calvin Stowe abroad to study the common schools and their methods, and Hattie's heart sank. Had she not been in "an interesting condition," she might have accompanied her husband on a glorious journey; somehow they would have found the money to meet her passage. Now she was to be without the mainstay of a husband when her first baby was born.

True, she was proud of her husband's standing as an educator, but the timing was cruel. Calvin was to sail from New York on the first of May; and with an additional commission from Lane to purchase foreign books for its library, he might not return for almost a year.

She needed Calvin at her side as never before, and yet it was he who was clinging to her. Always apt to shy away from any new venture, the big bulky man of thirty-four was in many ways a child to be regarded by his mite of a wife with maternal tenderness. She was frightened and sick with longing at the prospect of the long separation, but she dared not display this to Calvin.

Fate had played a curious trick upon one who had always imagined herself to be dependent and weak. It was forcing her to be resourceful and brave, and to face life instead of trying to hide from it. With her marriage, Hattie had grown up by leaps and by bounds. If she could not lose herself in love for a lover, she could feel deep affection and compassion for him.

With their last embrace upon the wharves of Cincinnati, she pressed a letter in his hand which was not to be unsealed until he was well out upon the ocean. They were

not the impassioned words of a bride of scarcely four
months and not yet twenty-five years of age; they contained a mature woman's wit and her wisdom:

> Now, my dear, that you are gone where you are out of the
> reach of my care, advice, and good management, it is fitting
> that you should have something under my hand and seal for
> your comfort and furtherance in the new world you are going
> to. Firstly, I must caution you to set your face as a flint
> against the 'cultivation of indigo' . . . dear one, you must
> give more way to hope than to memory. You are going to a
> new scene now, and one that I hope will be full of enjoy-
> ment for you. I want you to take the good of it.
> Only think of all you expect to see: the great libraries and
> beautiful paintings, fine churches. . . . My dear, I wish I
> were a man in your place; if I wouldn't have a grand time!

It would be seventeen years before Hattie went to Europe, and then it would be as an international celebrity.
Now she was a winsome, wistful wisp of a young woman
who, in her husband's absence, confessed to Georgianna
that she was like one keeping up a pathetic whistling in the
dark, "I look only to the present, and leave the future with
Him who has hitherto been so kind to me."

14

KITCHEN CREATIVITY

As HATTIE grew heavier with child, she was bravely writing to her bridegroom that he was not to worry; and she was reassuring him daily in a journal which she kept to forward to him once a month. Yet as she read his accounts of his adventures in Germany, she could not suppress envious sighs. Men could doff family responsibilities as easily as they might take off a cloak, while women stayed home and worried about finances and knit tiny garments.

Meanwhile, she was enjoying the close companionship of her two brothers, the ebullient Henry and poetic, musical Charles. She had moved into her father's house for the duration of Calvin's absence abroad; and she was keeping herself busy helping Aunt Esther run the household and assisting Henry who, temporarily, was editing a religious weekly, the *Journal*. Under its young and passionate editors, the publication soon departed from solely religious matters to take a stand, also, upon the question of mob violence.

Always, in Cincinnati, the slavery question lurked in the background ready to leap out from ambush; and in the sultry heat of that summer of 1836, tensions were again at a peak. Commercial buyers from the South filled the city, and a big convention was being held to promote a railroad that would link the fortunes of this border river city even more closely with those of the South. Thus, the publication here of an abolitionist paper by James G. Birney, an ex-slaveholder, was an ever-increasing source of chagrin.

One torrid July night, a mob took the problem into their own hands and, breaking into the establishment that was defiantly printing Birney's paper, wrecked the forms. Shockingly, it was not waterfront hoodlums but young men from the better classes who made up the bulk of this mob. So-called respectable citizens were winking, too, at further displays of lawlessness and permitting the mob madness to spread. While frightened Negroes vanished from the streets, lest they be run down and beaten, and the mobs vowed to have Birney's own skin, Hattie watched her brother Henry pouring lead into a mold to make bullets. She wrote in her daily journal:

> For a day or two we did not know but there would actually be war to the knife, as was threatened by the mob, and we really saw Henry depart with his pistols with daily alarm, only we were all too full of patriotism not to have sent every brother we had rather than not have had the principles of freedom and order defended.

Everyone was hotly taking sides, and Hattie observed, "I can easily see how such proceedings may make converts to abolitionism, for already my sympathies are strongly enlisted for Mr. Birney, and I hope that he will stand his ground and assert his rights."

Matters came to such a pass that Salmon P. Chase—the patrician young lawyer later to be Lincoln's Secretary of the Treasury, and currently a friend of Hattie's from the Semi-Colon Club—jeopardized his rising career and risked his life to bar the mob from Birney's hotel. The vividness of such personal impressions and experiences were to forge a mighty weapon in the pen which Hattie held in her hand, and which now she was using to write her first published remarks upon any phase of the slavery question.

For one so young, she was singularly wise and objective in her ingenious essay for Henry's publication, written under a masculine pseudonym. She could not go to Mr. Birney's aid with a pistol and police one of the windows of the printing plant, but she could spunkily declare that:

> Every man is glad of a mob that happens to fall in with his views, without considering that if the mob system gets once thoroughly running, it may go *against* as well as *for* them. . . . all lovers of good order must . . . accept of nothing as a good deed that is purchased by outrages endangering those rights of property and of free opinion which are the pride and treasure of every American citizen.

Hattie Beecher had become a fighter—all five feet of her—and she had need of her courage as she was about to have a child toward the end of September. The doctor had said apprehensively that she was small for the size of her burden, and both of them knew that the medical science of the time was often powerless to save either mother or child if complications developed. Many did not survive childbirth, but Hattie had resolutely put all such fears behind her. The severe disciplines of her Puritan upbringing had strengthened her inner fiber, and she could face the real tests with an heroic fortitude.

She longed for Calvin that she might cling to his hand. For nine months she had been nurturing this life; she had felt the stir of it, the tiny feet kicking, and now the pains in her abdomen were mounting with dizzying swiftness. Nature was at work with unabated zeal, and the faces of Aunt Esther and the doctor hovering over her swam through her mind.

And then, a thousand years later, it was over. Limp and exhausted, she lay back against the pillows remembering faintly that someone had said she had twins. Yes, it was true. Two tiny heads lay swaddled in the blanket beside her, twin daughters with mouths that were like freshly plucked rosebuds. Kissing each soft and downy head, the love welled up in Hattie's heart and overflowed. How good life could be when it doubled one's treasure!

Wouldn't Calvin be surprised? As soon as she felt strong enough, she wrote him ecstatic letters which he did not receive. What with his mail going astray and his passage over stormy winter seas lasting for two tempestuous months, it was mid-January before he reached New York and learned that he was the father of twins. February saw him back in Walnut Hills bouncing a five-month-old daughter upon either knee and insisting that the infant christened Isabella by her mother must be renamed Harriet Beecher Stowe. He approved of the name which had been chosen for the other daughter: Eliza Tyler Stowe. Twin girls . . . named for each of his wives.

With her husband's return, Hattie's domestic joy was complete. Now that her husband was regarded in Cincinnati circles as practically a world traveller who had seen all the sights, she could bask in his fame. And she was filled with plans for saving toward the purchase of new furniture and decorating the nursery. With twin babies under her care, she felt entitled to hire help which, in those days, was

cheap; and she was so fortunate as to engage a colored girl
of unusual ability and cleverness. The house sparkled and
meals were a dream of perfection, while Hattie wrote
steadily in spare moments to add to their income.

For a few short months before the storm clouds gathered, the Stowe's ménage was indeed home, sweet home.
Then their Negro servant turned out to be a fugitive slave
who had to be spirited away in the night by Henry and
Calvin to the safety of the "underground railway." And
presently the financial panic of 1837 swept away the fortune of the man who had been Lane's chief financial support; Lyman Beecher was practically penniless. To add to
their difficulties, Hattie was feeling extremely unwell; her
second pregnancy was to give her far more trouble than
her first.

As a climax to their problems—public and private—they
heard that crusading Edward Beecher had been killed with
the Reverend Elijah Lovejoy when a proslavery mob in
Alton, Illinois, wrecked the abolitionist press. Fortunately,
the rumor was unfounded; Hattie's brother turned out to
be alive and well, and in January she gave birth to a son,
Henry Ellis. Her mercurial spirits were again on the up-
swing when she wrote to Georgianna:

> Only think how long it is since I have written to you, and
> how changed I am since then—the mother of three children!
> Well, if I have not kept the reckoning of old times, let this
> last circumstance prove my apology, for I have been hand,
> heart and head-full since I saw you. . . . Well, Georgy, this
> marriage is—yes, I will speak well of it . . . for when I can
> stop and think long enough to discriminate my head from my
> heels, I must say that I think myself a fortunate woman in
> both husband and children. My children I would not change
> for all the ease, leisure, and pleasure I could have without

them. They are money on interest whose value will be constantly increasing. . . .

Whatever happened, her children were the joy of her
life—her children and her writing. Despite the fact that she
described herself to Georgianna playfully as "a mere
drudge with few ideas beyond babies and housekeeping,"
she had been selling bits and pieces at twenty to twenty-
five dollars each to such sentimental annuals as *Souvenir*
and *Affection's Gift*. In a day when living was so cheap
that meat was only five or ten cents a pound and servant
girls could be had for less than a dollar a week, Hattie
could, with her writing, afford to splurge upon both a
nurse for her children and kitchen help for herself.

The Stowe's continued unsettled financial situation had
made Hattie determine to become a professional writer;
and now, with the servants, she was able to devote three
hours a day to this work. She was learning how to write to
please editors—if not to suit herself; and as she informed
her friends when they began to see her name coming out
here and there, she was doing it for "the pay."

The economic pressure had a benefit: it was good discipline for one who had never been able to organize her
time successfully, and it was excellent practice. She no
longer waited for inspiration to strike but sat down at the
scheduled hour and, picking up her pen, hoped that some
thought would flow.

With her first earnings from her writing after marriage,
she had bought pillows and a feather bed; and now, whenever a new mattress or carpet were needed, she went off
to her desk. It seemed to her that she had discovered
"the philosopher's stone" by which ancient alchemists attempted to turn dross into gold.

As a result of both the financial panic and the Weld

agitation which had diverted many students to the radical
new Oberlin College that was to fill the pulpits of the
Middle West with its graduates, not one freshman appeared that fall to enroll in Lane Seminary. Upperclass-
men numbered only a handful, and temperamental Calvin
Stowe was ready to bury the whole once-promising institution. As so often in time of crisis, he was overcome by
melancholia and retired to his bed. His father-in-law was
made of far sterner stuff and, indomitable as always, went
out to comb the bushes. Returning with twelve prospec-
tive preachers, Lyman Beecher cried, "Wake up, Stowe!
I've brought ye twelve students. Get up and wash, and eat
bread, and prepare to have a good class."

Calvin Stowe groaned. Here he was—eminent scholar
and recent European traveller—bogged down in a school
that had barely kept its head above water since the Weld
agitation and the adverse publicity which had termed it a
"Bastile of oppression." Now he had married Beecher's
daughter, had three children, and, so far as he could see,
was trapped for the rest of his life. He could never support
her—he was not cut out to be a family man—and so forth
and so on.

Calvin Stowe was haunted by specters far more real than
the fantasies of his childhood; he let adversity prey on his
mind where it sharpened the wits of Hattie and her father.
She had not been strong since the birth of her third child,
but she was writing steadily, propelled by nervous energy
and dire necessity. It was becoming all too apparent that
what Calvin Stowe lacked was backbone and that his little
wife must supply it for the two of them.

Where Calvin Stowe saw defeat written large in his
book, a true Beecher did not know the meaning of the
word. One member of this notable family egged on the
other, and times were never so serious that they could not

take time out to have a good chuckle. Kate too was beset with financial difficulties, but her arrival upon the scene was like a fresh and cheerful breeze. Whether it was she or a friend who recorded the scene of Hattie's current literary activities was never made clear, but Kate had the wit to do this memorable sketch:

"Come, Harriet," said I, as I found her tending one baby and watching two others just able to walk, "where is that piece for the *Souvenir* which I promised the editor . . .? You have only this one day to finish it, and have it I must. . . .

"As to house cleaning, you can defer it one day longer; and as to baby's teeth, there is to be no end to them, as I can see. No, no; today that story must be ended. There Frederick has been sitting by Ellen for more than a month now, and she has been turning and blushing until I am sure it is time to go to her relief. . . . Two dollars a page, my dear, and you can write a page in fifteen minutes!"

"But, my dear, here is a baby in my arms and two little pussies by my side, and there is a great baking down in the kitchen, and there is a "new girl" for help. . . . It is really out of the question, you see."

"I see no such thing. I do not know what genius is given for, if it is not help a woman out of a scrape. Come, set your wits to work. . . ."

"Well, but the kitchen affairs?"

"We can manage them, too. You know you can write anywhere and anyhow. Just take your seat at the kitchen table. . . ." I carried my point. In ten minutes she was seated; a table with flour . . . and lard on one side, a dresser with eggs, pork, and beans . . . near her an oven heating, and beside her a dark-skinned nymph awaiting orders.

"Here, Harriet," said I, "you can write on this atlas in your lap; no matter how the writing looks, I will copy it."

"Well, well," said she, with a resigned sort of amused look. "Mina, you may do what I told you, while I write a few minutes, till it is time to mold the bread. Where is the inkstand?"

"Here it is, close by, on the top of the tea kettle," said I.

At this Mina giggled, and we both laughed to see her merriment at our literary proceedings. I began to overhaul the portfolio to find the right sheet.

"Here it is," said I. "Here is Frederick sitting by Ellen, glancing at her brilliant face, and saying something about 'guardian angel,' and all that—you remember?"

"Yes, yes," said she, falling into a muse, as she attempted to recover the thread of her story.

"Ma'am, shall I put the pork on the top of the beans?" asked Mina.

"Come, come," said Harriet, laughing. "You see how it is. Mina is a new hand and cannot do anything without me to direct it. We must give up writing for today."

"No, no, let us have another trial. You can dictate as easily as you can write. Come, I will set the baby in this clothes-basket and . . . you shall dictate and I will write. Now this is the place where you left off: you were describing the scene between Ellen and her lover. . . ."

"Mina, pour a little milk into this pearlash," said Harriet. . . .

"Here," said I, "let me direct Mina about these matters and write awhile yourself."

Harriet took the pen and patiently set herself to work. For a while my culinary knowledge and skill were proof to all Mina's investigating inquiries, and they did not fail until I saw two pages completed. . . .

"I am ready to write," said I. "The last sentence was: What is this life to one who has suffered as I have?"

"Shall I put in the brown or the white bread first?" said Mina.

"The brown first," said Harriet.

"What is this life to one who has suffered as I have?" said I.

Harriet brushed the flour off her apron and sat down for a moment in a muse. Then she dictated as follows:

"Under the breaking of my heart I have borne up. I have borne up under all that tries a woman. . . ."

"Ma'am, shall I put ginger into this pumpkin?" queried Mina.

"No, you may let it alone just now," replied Harriet. She then proceeded:

"I know my duty to my children. I see the hour must come . . . they are my last earthly comfort."

"Ma'am, what shall I do with these eggshells and all this truck here?" interrupted Mina.

"Put them in the pail by you," answered Harriet.

"They are my last earthly comfort," said I. "What next?"

She continued to dictate: "You must take them away. It may be—perhaps it must be—that I shall soon follow, but the breaking heart of a wife still pleads——"

"How much longer must the gingerbread stay in?" inquired Mina.

"Five minutes," said Harriet.

"A little longer, a little longer," I repeated in a dolorous tone, and we burst into a laugh.

Thus we went on, cooking, writing, nursing, and laughing, till I finally accomplished my object. The piece was finished, copied, and the next day sent to the editor.

15

THE PAINFUL YEARS

Hattie's life was shot through with tears and with laughter, with the shouts of children at play, with large hopes deferred and small mercies realized; and she had the peculiar ability to reflect it in the mirror of words. The racy humor of Calvin's New England stories were forming the basis for some of her best character sketches along with the ever-present servant problem and the grim godliness of the Puritan Sabbath which she viewed with a wit that kept even her religious idealism warm and human.

Often she wrote as formlessly as she would talk to a friend, and as casually, about whatever came into her head. She was impatient, not caring for the discipline of literary construction but throwing out words in a breathless spate from which ideas and people and action somehow emerged. She adored children, animals, flowers and could write about them with exquisite detail. Loving and submissive, she had yet a streak of New England granite; she was simple, she was complex, she was myriad kinds of woman.

From the time she married Calvin she was up to her elbows in life and its realities—a baby every year or two, a difficult husband with whom to cope. Hers was a living, breathing world where the passion and intensity of human relationships mingled with soft gentle undercurrents; and she could write about them in moving terms which her readers understood.

From her experience of the common lot she was developing a skill at communication that, when the time was ripe, would have extraordinary power to reach the mind and the conscience of millions. Meanwhile, much of her writing consisted of sermonizing parables and other forms of Victorian soothing syrup because it was what the editors wanted from her.

Nevertheless, a vein of truth and intelligence ran through all of her work. Consciously and unconsciously, she was always taking mental notes to be stored away and taken out for later translation. She listened acutely as her perceptive brother Charles shared with her his firsthand observations of the slave trade and the slave markets as he had seen them in New Orleans, where he had gone as a brokerage clerk. Many of his tales were so hideous that they chilled her blood, and from them were to emerge scenes and characters in her first novel, among them the sinister and sadistic figure of Simon Legree.

Later, when she came to write her book, she would find Topsy in a mischievous black imp in her Sunday School class; and she would draw Miss Ophelia from Aunt Esther who, kind as she was, failed to understand anyone who did not think as she did and whose skin was not white.

Living in Cincinnati through these turbulent years, Hattie was obtaining a broad view of the slavery problem. It was complex and would not yield to such a quick solution as the abolitionists were urging. To her mind they were "Like all asserters of pure abstract right as applied to human affairs . . . regarded as a species of moral mono-maniacs who, in consideration of one class of interests and wrongs, had lost sight of all proportion and all good judg-ment. Both in church and state they were looked upon as 'those that troubled Israel.' "

She had come to look upon slavery as an evil for which the South was not solely responsible. Though folk in northern cities less strategically located than Cincinnati were still trying vainly to ignore the whole problem, the whole nation must share in the blame. Hattie would not have been a true Beecher had she not had an earnest desire for reform; but as for slavery: "It was a general saying among conservative and sagacious people that this subject was a dangerous one to investigate; and that nobody could begin to read or think about it without becoming prac-tically insane. . . ."

As a later generation might tremble before the fears of nuclear destruction, so Hattie was to write in her intro-duction to *Uncle Tom's Cabin* that in the 1840's slavery was "a sort of general impression on her mind, as upon that of many humane people in those days, that the subject was so dark and painful a one, so involved in difficulty and obscurity, so utterly beyond human hope or help, that it was of no use to read, or think, or distress oneself about it. . . ."

In a way, Hattie too was enslaved, trapped by life to carry burdens so heavy that she often sank under their weight. The cry of the oppressed—how often she herself had uttered it from the depths of her soul. A neuralgic pain settled in her eyes and kept her from writing, made any light painful. And then, with the birth of her fourth child, Frederick William, she was confined to her bed sev-eral months while the Stowe's expenses kept mounting.

And yet, though the year of 1840 had been particularly fraught with trouble, she was able to regard herself as still "greatly blessed." The children were thriving and "came to more" than the care of them. And she had a husband who could say to her and mean it that "there is no woman like you in this wide world."

Though unworldly Calvin Stowe was no money-maker and bitter poverty was seldom far from their door, the bond between husband and wife was close and warm. In this, Hattie had more than many a woman who was petted and indulged and had every luxury from her husband but love.

Her nervous and physical energy finally restored after her baby's birth, Hattie was up and flying again with a beat of wings swift as a bird's. Presently a great encouragement came to her, the obscure writer out in the provinces, churning out manuscripts only for "the pay." Sister Kate, who was one to get about and have a shrewd eye for contacts, had showed some of her work to the rising publishing house of Harper's in New York; and they were so impressed with them that they were offering to bring out a book of Hattie's sketches. The astonished author picked a name for this volume—*The Mayflower*—and forthwith determined that she must go East to see the editors.

Leaving her household in charge of Aunt Esther and taking little Harriet with her, Hattie left for New York with name and fame written large before her eyes. Stopping at various other editorial offices, she was finding many new markets for her work; and Calvin shared her high hopes. The little Cincinnati housewife was marked by fate to become a literary woman, he wrote to her:

> Get a good stock of health and brush up your mind. Drop the *E* out of your name. It only encumbers it and interferes

with the flow of euphony. Write yourself fully and always Harriet Beecher Stowe, which is a name euphonious, flowing, and full of meaning. Then my word for it, your husband will lift up his head in the gate, and your children will rise up and call you blessed.

From her vantage point in the East and her present prospects of literary success, Hattie felt that she must assert herself, as never within her home precincts. "If I am to write, I must have a room to myself which shall be *my* room."

She could no longer afford to be interrupted by constant annoyances. It was impossible for her to concentrate where there was "all the setting of tables . . . and dressing and washing of children, and everything else going on, and the continual falling of soot and coal dust. . . ." She had in mind a little-used chilly chamber where they could put up a stove; she could have her plants in there, and shut the door, and be comfortable.

For a change, Hattie was acting like Mrs. Independence; but Calvin was so lonesome for her that he was willing to consider even such a rank extravagance as she was suggesting. It had never occurred to him that she too needed privacy for her own cerebrations. He himself was always cozy in the parlor when he worked, frowning at her when she came in to occupy so much as a corner away from the demands of the children. The main thing now was for her to come home as quickly as possible:

The fact is I cannot live without you, and if we were not so prodigious poor I would come for you at once. . . . Who else has so much talent with so little self-conceit; so much reputation with so little affectation . . . so much enterprise with so little extravagance; so much tongue with so little

scold; so much sweetness with so little softness; so much of
so many things and so little of so many other things?

Calvin Stowe had drawn a loving portrait of his wife,
and it was almost as good as a courtship all over again. "If
you were not already my dearly beloved husband I should
certainly fall in love with you," Hattie responded. Absence
was stirring up the old embers, and Hattie was filled with
bright resolutions. She knew that her absent-mindedness
and forgetfulness annoyed her husband, and she would try
to improve.

But alas for the Stowes and their splendid intentions!
The honeymoon was over soon after Hattie's return to Cincinnati, and the years continued to grind exceedingly hard
upon both of them. "I am sick of the smell of sour milk
and sour meat, and sour everything, and then the clothes
will not dry, and no wet thing does, and everything smells
mouldy; and altogether I feel as if I never wanted to eat
again. . . ."

Hattie was well into her years of despair, and far from
molding the mind of the West with the publication of her
The Mayflower, as Calvin had enthusiastically prophesied.
Hattie had little more than a book in hard-cover to present
to friends and relatives with her autograph. To meet expenses, she was back at her desk again, turning out bits of
hack work for "the pay." Household cares and expenses
overwhelmed the Stowe household as Calvin's modest salary went unpaid for months at a time. It was almost too
much for Hattie; she had barely rallied from the shock of
her brother George's accidental death when she gave birth
to her fifth child, Georgianna May.

Sick in body and soul from the disillusionments and de-
pressions of trying to make a good life somehow, Hattie
had days when she felt "an indistinct terror, as if father,

brothers, husband, any or all, might be just about to sink."
Then it was that Calvin Stowe took over and, to Hattie's
surprise, became model house-father and nurse.

> You would laugh to see him in his spectacles gravely
> marching the little troupe in their night-gowns up to bed,
> tagging after them as he says, like an old hen after a flock of
> ducks. . . .

Hattie recorded the family scene upon the eve of her
departure for Vermont. Her health had become so poor
that the whole family was alarmed, and somehow money
had come from "an unknown hand" to permit her to go to
Brattleboro. Here she might take the famous "water-cure,"
with Kate as sprightly company for a part of her stay. Hattie would be away from Cincinnati for almost a year.

God was good—Hattie was convinced of it as she returned to her household, once more buoyant in body and
soul. "All this shows the care of the Father, and encourages
me to rejoice and hope in Him."

She had need of such faith in the difficult years that still
lay ahead of her. She was again pregnant and afflicted with
the neuralgic pain that made any writing—outside of a few
letters—out of the question. Her talents lay fallow, her pen
almost idle.

With the birth of their sixth child, Samuel Charles, she
went up in health and spirits where Calvin went down. He
had not had a real vacation in fifteen years, and it was
more than high time. The "water-cure" in Vermont
should solve whatever problems he had, and Hattie
bravely assured him that she could manage without him.
His sabbatical year of leave from Lane was long overdue.

In the interim, she would keep boarders, open a small
school, do whatever she could to keep the pot boiling there

in Cincinnati. A husband and wife stood together through sunshine and storm—or so she had been taught to believe. Calvin had sustained her devotedly during her own long illness, and he must have a similar chance to recupererate from the stresses and strains incident to their family life. Six children, and practically no money.

With the newest baby in her arms and the rest of their flock clustered about, she and Calvin bid a good-bye. Hattie was thirty-seven and glad of it. "I like to grow old and have six children and cares endless . . . were they gone I should ask myself, What now remains to be done? They are my work. . . ."

She surrounded her children with the cloak of her love, thrown heedlessly and joyously about them. And she tried to be equally protective of her husband when, almost a year after his departure, cholera again broke out in Cincinnati in epidemic proportions. She was facing this ghastly specter alone.

At the news, Calvin was anxious to return, but she would not hear of it. With his system made sensitive by the water-cure treatment, he could be among the first to fall victim. (Besides, had Calvin ever been useful in any emergency?)

Neither Hattie nor any of the children were as yet sick and they might escape. Yet, in the journal which Hattie kept to send to her husband, she admitted that this week of June 29 had been unusually fatal, and that drivers of hearses barely had time to unharness their horses. The night air of that summer of 1849 was peculiarly oppressive as it rose to Walnut Hills from the pestilential and terrified city only two miles away; it was of the "deathly kind that seems so like lead on the brain and soul."

Better to stay where they were than try to flee, she decided. The stagecoaches leaving Cincinnati were bulging, and few steamboats dared to risk mutiny from their crews to make a landing. While half the city was bent on carousing, filling the taverns to escape from the panic in their souls, the other half were on their knees praying. "Oh, Lord deliver us in Thy everlasting mercy. . . ."

Death walked the streets and the country lanes like the Black Death of the Middle Ages, while Hattie did her best to refrain from hysteria. She kept her house cool and quiet and her voice low when gentlemen stopped by to report the number of deaths in this family or that one. As the vast panorama of tragedy spread about her, she was keeping her perspective. They were still all in good health, and she was trying to maintain an optimistic, cheerful frame of mind, going out into the dawn to hear the awakening song of the birds.

What would be, would be; it was barely possible that the Stowes might be spared. Looking down at her children each night as they lay in their beds, rosy-cheeked in the lamplight, she wondered whether it was wicked to feel a fierce love. She yearned to place herself between them and all harm, preferring to offer herself as a sacrifice if that were the will of the Lord.

And then there came the dreadful night when baby Charley tossed in his sleep and cried out, when she took him into her bed and tried to tell herself that this must be a mere childish ailment and no cause for alarm. Taking him to one of the overworked doctors next day, she returned home with a heavy heart. That night she was awakened from a troubled sleep by one of the boarders who burst into her room with the news that eleven-year-old Henry was vomiting. She soon brought him relief and discovered that, wonder of wonders, Charley seemed to be very much better. He was cross, and she and her faithful nurse Anna rejoiced to hear how he scolded.

Like other households, theirs was now in a state of siege,

with Hattie and Anna near prostrate with worry and exhaustion. While the children mourned their pet dog Daisy who had died in a spasm, the twins helped their mother make a shroud and a burial cap for the devoted old colored woman who, only yesterday, had come to do their washing.

Ten days after his first attack, baby Charley took a sudden turn for the worse, and there was no hope of saving him. He would be gone before Calvin could reach them, and on July 26 Hattie wrote to her husband:

> At last it is over, and our dear little one is gone from us . . . my beautiful, loving, gladsome baby, so loving, so sweet, so full of life and hope and strength—now lies, shrouded pale and cold. . . . Never was he anything to me but a comfort. . . . Many an anxious night have I held him to my bosom and felt the sorrow and loneliness pass out of me with the touch of his little warm hands. Yet I have just seen him in his death agony, looked on his imploring face when I could not . . . do one thing to mitigate his cruel suffering . . . I write as though there were no sorrow like my sorrow, yet there has been in this city, as in the land of Egypt, scarce a house without its dead. . . .

It was the cry of an anguished mother separated forever from her child, and it was the theme that would run through the whole of *Uncle Tom's Cabin*. Hattie knew how a slave mother must feel when her baby was torn from her bosom and sold by a ruthless master. How a frantic mother could flee upon the wings of the wind if there were a chance that she and her little one might be saved. Hattie would be writing out of her own devastation and helplessness, dipping her pen into the blood of a grief-stricken heart.

16

ON THE MOVE

WHEN CALVIN returned, it was with the welcome news
that with spring the Stowes would be moving back East.
Suddenly the sultry air of Cincinnati cleared with fresh
hope and a fresh breeze blowing straight from the state of
Maine. After nearly eighteen years, Hattie would be saying
farewell to the booming, brawling, flamboyant river city
that had never seemed really home to her. It would be
good-bye also to the colorful steamboats and the excitement of the wharves, and to the handsome brick residences
where the members of the Semi-Colon Club had welcomed
her with an openhandedness that mingled the hospitality
of the West with that of the South.

Hattie had been shaken out of her narrow New England
ways, never to return to them as a zealot or prig; and she
had acquired a breadth of vision that never would leave
her. She knew the world that existed outside of New England, the churning, ambitious, ever-moving mass of folk
with a dozen heritages that were different from hers. And

yet it was a relief to be going back to a land where families had roots and had lived behind the same fanlighted doorways for many generations; it would be good to hear the nasal twang of the New England voices.

Despite his loyalty to his wife's father, Calvin Stowe had grown weary of trying to eke out a living in the backwater that Lane had become; and he had accepted an offer from his old alma mater, Bowdoin College. True, his salary would be only $1,500 a year, but he would be back in the academic circles where he belonged and where his record and his contacts had been brilliant. He had been a classmate of Franklin Pierce, Nathaniel Hawthorne, and Henry Wadsworth Longfellow.

Whatever the change might hold for them, it would be a change for the better, Hattie thought, trying to rise above her grief over the baby's death to renew her relations with editors and do her first writing in months. The move would be expensive, and the whole family was threadbare. Here in Cincinnati it had become impossible to conceal their poverty-stricken plight, but new clothes would help them put up a respectable front in the East. Hattie had her pride, and she'd no mind to arrive there looking poor as a church mouse.

With a fresh incentive, she sped about her household tasks and her sewing, picking up her pen to dash off a piece or two and working far into the night. Being busy was a blessing that kept her from brooding, but there was a question as to whether she should keep Charley's baby clothes or give them away. As in *Uncle Tom's Cabin:*

> Mrs. Bird slowly opened the drawer. There were the little coats . . . piles of aprons, and rows of small stockings; and even a pair of little shoes, worn and rubbed at the toes. . . . There was a toy horse and wagon. . . . She sat down . . .

and wept till the tears fell through her fingers into the
drawer.

When Hattie discovered that she was to have another
baby who would need every bootee and bonnet, it called
for a drastic change in their plans for the move. Her confinement would take place around the middle of July, and
Calvin had learned that he would be unable to leave Lane
until June. Such close timing would be precarious for Hattie; she must start off in April to make the long journey on
her own by riverboat, canalboat, and rail. Yes, she would
go on ahead to make all the arrangements: find a house,
gather up bits of furniture, and get settled before the baby
was due to arrive.

She was a changed woman from the timid bride who had
been afraid to risk her "delicate condition" and go East
with Calvin to see him off for Europe. Time and again
through the years of her marriage to a man who fumbled
and who often disappointed her, she had been thrown
upon her own resources; and the lines of character in her
face had sharpened. Publicly she gave the appearance of
leaning upon her husband, as a good Victorian wife
should, but privately she knew that her reliance was chiefly
upon herself and upon God.

Despite her trials in Cincinnati, she was carrying rare
riches away with her: self-confidence, skill as a professional
writer, and the seeds of a novel. And she had her children,
three of whom were to be her travelling companions:
Georgie, a tomboy of seven, and lively ten-year-old Fred-
die, plus her namesake Harriet who, at fourteen, could
assist her mother should disaster befall. As Hattie stood on
the deck of the side-wheeler moving away from Cincinnati,
the tired corners of her soft mouth lifted and her eyes were
alight.

By staying with relatives en route and sitting up all night on occasion among the cinders of the railroad cars, Hattie figured thriftily that the trip for the four of them could be made for around seventy-five dollars. She was looking forward to seeing her brother Henry Ward in Brooklyn Heights, where he had zoomed to wealth and popularity in his Plymouth Church pulpit. "Henry's people are more than ever in love with him," she wrote to her husband, "and have raised his salary to $3300, and given him a beautiful horse and carriage worth $600."

Visiting in Henry's fine home, she was ever more proud and adoring of him. He had taken a dramatic stand against slavery, and was staging sensational "slave auctions." The proposed Fugitive Slave Law was a disgrace to the country, he told her, and he was using every possible means to arouse his influential congregation.

All through the East—at Henry's house and again at her brother Edward's in Boston—Hattie found tensions at a peak. They were tensions such as she had known for years in Cincinnati, but now they were sweeping the country as a result of the furious debates in Congress over the Compromise of 1850.

With the discovery of gold in California two years previously, thousands had rushed into the territory newly acquired from Mexico, and now California was requesting admission to the Union as a "free" state. Alarmed at the growing power of the North and its opposition to the extension of slavery, many southerners were shouting that it was time to secede. Their leader was the redoubtable old warrior John C. Calhoun of South Carolina. As the country hovered on the brink of Civil War, able but aging Henry Clay of Kentucky had come forth with a compromise that many, north and south, declared to be infamous.

Both sides were to make concessions; and for the North,

the bitterest was to agree to a more potent Fugitive Slave
Law. The third giant of the Senate, Daniel Webster of
Massachusetts, agreed with Clay. The nation had little
choice; either it must accept compromise, or it would have
war. He was as much a traitor to his section of the country
as Clay was to his, the angry voices cried, as—at great personal and political sacrifice—Webster lent the might of his
oratory to the preservation of the United States of America.

Absorbed in her domestic problems and considering
politics to be the business of menfolks, Hattie listened with
little comment to the discussions going on all about her in
the East. She had heard heated arguments pro and con
before she left Cincinnati, but here they were even more
passionately weighted. The abolitionist poet John Green-
leaf Whittier expressed a general feeling in his denuncia-
tion of Webster: "From those great eyes the soul has
fled."

If Hattie had hoped she might avoid profoundly disturbing talk about slavery by coming East, she had stepped
from the frying pan into the fire. But at the moment, she
had her own tribulations. With her baby now less than two
months away, she was exhausted by the time she reached
Boston, where she was faced with the necessity of finding
enough furnishings to set up housekeeping in Maine with
but a hundred and fifty dollars to spend. Yet with characteristic bravery she wrote to her husband, "I am strong in
spirit, and God who has been with me in so many straits
will not forsake me now."

Once she reached her destination in Brunswick, she was
enclosed by warm arms. Mrs. Upham, wife of one of the
Bowdoin professors, opened her sweet, quiet home to the
weary little mother and her children, and gave her a week
of perfect rest. Meanwhile, a house was found for the

Stowes upon one of the best residential streets; the rent was cheap because it had been long unoccupied and was badly in need of repairs. The old place was drearier and damper than ever when Hattie first saw it in the midst of a northeaster storm; but it had a sound New England simplicity of architecture and could be whipped into shape.

Hattie had a formidable task to accomplish before her baby arrived; but later on she could give an amusing account of her experiences in a letter to her sister-in-law. In the first place, there had been a doleful missive from Calvin saying "he is sick abed and all but dead; don't ever expect to see his family again; wants to know how I shall manage, in case I am left a widow; wonders at my courage; knows we shall get into debt and never get out; thinks I am very sanguine; warns me to be prudent, as there won't be much to live on in case of his death, etc. etc. etc. I read the letter and poke it into the stove and proceed. . . ."

All day long in the ensuing weeks, she was running from one thing to another: showing the neighborhood handy man how to nail down the carpet straight instead of crooked, sending the children running to the store for soap to wash windows, showing a woman how to make a sofa and cover it with bits and pieces of cloth, finding screws for the bedsteads and getting them set up in place.

Her ingenuity was taxed to the utmost as her head kept up with her heels. There was not a cistern in the cellar to supply the kitchen with water, not a sink, not a pump. Racking her brains as to what to do about getting a cistern without spending a large sum for it, she bought two great hogsheads from one of the factories, only to find that the only door to the cellar led down a long flight of stairs far too narrow to admit them. Oh, for some chivalrous knight who might breach the foundations! Failing one, she resorted to flattery. Surely one of the good Yankee coopers was sufficiently master of his craft to take both of the barrels apart and, carrying them into the cellar stave by stave, set them up again to stand "as innocent and quiet as could be."

Dumbfounded by her cleverness in surmounting this difficulty, one of the college professors who stopped by to check on her progress shook his head and remarked, "Well, nothing can beat a willful woman." She had further need of her wiles in persuading her eccentric landlord, Mr. Titcomb, to build her a sink so that she could order a pump; he was a man who refused to be hurried. A carpenter by trade and related to the best families in town, he lived in a veritable curiosity shop. Here, among whale teeth, ancestral portraits, and old spinning wheels, he sat rocking back and forth, ready to pass the time of day for many an hour. Concealing her impatience, Hattie would talk first of the news of the day, then of the weather or the prospects for a millenium until—as though the thought had just struck her—she would mention the sink.

"I think there's no hurry. I believe we are going to have a dry time now, so that you could not catch any water," Titcomb would drawl.

To a woman approaching confinement, every moment was precious. With the help of the Martha-by-the-day whom she had hired, she made "two sofas, or lounges, a barrel chair, divers bedspreads, pillowcases, pillows, bolsters, mattresses; we painted rooms; we re-varnished furniture; we—what *didn't* we do?"

Then came the first of July and, at long last, the sink, followed by Calvin and the rest of her brood. Hattie had finished her settling barely in time, for her baby was born on the eighth of July. He was her seventh child, and he was to be her last—another Charley, Charles Edward. With magnificent understatement, she wrote, "I was really glad for an excuse to lie in bed, for I was full tired, I can assure you."

Once she had time to look about her and catch her breath, she found Brunswick delightful. It was a shipbuilding town, redolent with the smell of freshly cut timbers and with the fragrance of pines warmed by the fragrance of the summer sun that danced across the waters of inlets and bays. It was a new experience for Hattie to live not far from the sea and to picnic beside one of the bays where the children could swim while she dreamed, dreamed of faraway places with an ardor she had not known since her youth. She was thirty-nine now; but as the sunbonnet slipped down over her shoulders and her brown curls blew about her face with heedless abandon in the breeze that brought pink to her cheeks, she could feel almost girlish. No matter what her husband's misgivings might be, she somehow was sure that the best years of their lives lay ahead of them.

17

"I WILL WRITE THAT THING"

CALVIN WAS worried and disgruntled that summer. Lane Seminary had refused to release him until they could find a replacement to fill his post; and recently a far better offer than the one here at Bowdoin had come to him from Andover Seminary, the best theological school in the East. It built up his pride to have three schools eager to have him on the faculty, but he was in a quandary. There was nothing for it but to return to Cincinnati temporarily, leaving his family in their usual poverty-stricken state.

To make ends meet, Hattie did the work of two servants and opened a small school in their home; in the invigorating air of Maine, she had become a whirlwind of energy. Organizing her time, she was writing more than she ever would have thought possible—journalistic pieces, sermonettes, potboilers of whatever type occurred to her.

She had no time to write letters to anyone but her husband and various editors, but she had revived her interest in novels and was reading Sir Walter Scott aloud to her

children each night. *Kenilworth* and *The Abbot,* it was
romantic fiction pulsating with drama and colorful action,
beside which her own little New England sketches seemed
pallid as tea.

Why had she never attempted a novel? Was it because
she did not have the ability or the discipline to sustain a
long effort and paint a big canvas? She was impatient, that
was part of the trouble, hasty about writing down her ideas
and sending them off without a second glance, hoping always that some editor would accept them and not be slow
in "the pay." H-m-m. Putting another comforter on her
bed against the penetrating chill of the crisp starry nights,
she lay long awake pondering.

For some time now she had been constantly pursued and
even haunted by the notion that she should be doing
something important, that the true coin of her life—outside of her husband and children—was being spent upon
trifles. Futility . . . futility . . . all was futility and frus-
tration when she longed to utter a significant cry for humanity. It seemed to her that she had betrayed the little
girl who, long ago in the old Litchfield meetinghouse, had
been stirred with patriotic fervor and had determined to
make a declaration of her own when she grew up.

To be sure, Hattie had had excuses aplenty for post-
poning a major undertaking, whatever form it might assume. She could be deaf to the clamor of her times when
each one of her days was filled with interruptions and demands. There would come knocks at her door ". . . once
for the fish-man to buy a codfish; once to see a man who
had brought me some barrels of apples; once to see a
book-man; then to see Mrs. Upham, to see about a drawing
I promised to make for her; then to nurse the baby; then
into the kitchen to make a chowder for dinner. . . ."

Then she was back at her desk again "for nothing but

deadly determination enables me ever to write; it is row-
ing against wind and tide." She was truly humble about
her achievements to date; and it came as a surprise to her
when Sarah Josepha Hale, editor of the popular *Godey's
Lady's Book,* asked to include a sketch of her in the magazine, among a group of woman writers. It was in Novem-
ber of 1850 that she answered the noted editor with characteristic candor:

> I was quite amused at your letter wholly innocent as I am
> to any pretensions to rank among "distinguished women."
> I read it to my little tribe of little folks assembled around the
> evening center table to let them know what a distinguished
> honor had befallen their mama. The idea of the daguerreo-
> type especially was quite droll, and I diverted myself some-
> what with figuring the astonishment of the children should
> the well-known visage of their mother loom out of the pages
> of a book before their astonished eyes.
>
> But in sober sadness, having reflected duly and truly on my
> past life, it is so thoroughly uneventful and uninteresting
> that I do not see how any thing can be done for me in the
> way of a sketch. My sister Catherine has lived much more of a
> life—and done more that can be told than I whose course and
> employment have always been retired and domestic. . . . the
> greater portion of my time and strength has been spent in the
> necessary but unpoetic duties of the family. These details you
> can throw into two or three lines—as great a space as I should
> have any claim to occupy in such company. . . ."

For one whose future was veiled, Hattie was not speaking with false modesty. Neither she nor anyone else could
foresee that in less than a year from the date of her letter to
Mrs. Hale, the name of one who had lived in comparative
obscurity would be upon thousands of lips.

Scarcely a household she visited here in Maine was not discussing the recently passed Fugitive Slave Law, some with an indignation that was equal to the Stowes' and others with a resignation that appalled her. These last declared that all opposition to the new Law endangered the Union, and even some of the most tenderhearted insisted that it was the duty of every American "to close their eyes, ears, and hearts to the harrowing details of slavery." They were trying to silence all arguments against it and even to assist slaveowners to recover the fugitives because "this was the law."

Such as they could not possibly know what slavery was like, know what they were defending, Hattie thought, quiet in company, ominously still and abstracted. If they had only seen what she had in Cincinnati, heard all the stories, met so saintly a colored man as "Father" Henson at her brother Edward's in Boston, their attitudes would be very different. Flogged by a brutal master until his shoulders were broken, Henson had been crippled for life; yet he had forgiven his tormentor and prayed for his soul.

It was shocking to Hattie that here in Maine, as in much of America, most folks were hushed down. "All the Capitol, all the political power and much of the Ecclesiastical is against agitation of this subject." Her mail from Boston was bringing her accounts of terrible abuses there, of long-resident Negro families ruthlessly broken up, of men frozen to death in their flight through pathless forests en route to Canada. Some Boston clergymen were actually speaking in defense of the "men-stealers."

With every letter from Boston, Hattie felt her gorge rising. Both her brother Edward and his wife were confirmed abolitionists; and though Hattie had always eschewed politics as unladylike, she was becoming convinced that she must enter the arena in some fashion. She could never again face herself if she did not try to respond to Mrs. Edward Beecher's plea:

Hattie, if I could use a pen as you can, I would write something to make this whole nation feel what an accursed thing slavery is.

Her older children were never to forget how their mother, reading the letter aloud to the cozy family circle, rose to her feet at this passage and, with an expression that stamped itself indelibly on their minds, crushed the letter in her hand and cried, "I will write something. I will if I live!"

The "if I live" did not alarm them; mother was not about to die. The expression was a common one, a Victorian foible in an age that deemed it proper for ladies to pretend to be frail and not long for this world. Perhaps, too, it had an element of superstition about it, like knocking on wood.

Hattie's message went back to Boston as the December blizzards closed in around Brunswick. "I will write that thing." With the snowdrifts piled high, Hattie went sledding with the children and helped them make plans for a Christmas that would not be Puritanical: " . . . everyone collecting their little gifts with wonderful mystery and secrecy."

But how should she go about executing "that thing"? A dozen plans came to her mind, and she discarded them while the baby whimpered and the twins hammered out scales and marches on the piano next door to her study. Cold weather was never her best time for writing; she welcomed the spring and the summer. Here in Maine, sitting close to an airtight stove that did not warm the floor, her feet froze as her brain torpified. Her thoughts never ran free "until the sap begins to rise in the trees."

When her brother Henry Ward arrived toward the end of January, he would not hear of further delay. Hours late on the train which now ran from Boston, he made his way to her door in a driving snowstorm and, sweeping the flakes from his cape with a dramatic flourish, settled down with her beside the stove to talk from midnight till dawn. Edward had told him that she intended to write something about slavery, and he was urging her to make haste. She with her pen and he with his preaching must agitate, agitate, agitate.

Oh, dear . . . oh, dear, whatever would Calvin say if he knew what she was proposing to do? He knew that she was planning an article for the antislavery publication *National Era* on the capacities of liberated Negroes to take care of themselves, and he had raised no objections. But knowing herself as she did, Hattie could not be sure that the subject would not gallop away with her like a runaway horse.

She had accumulated so much material in the course of the years that she did not know quite where to start. For days, while the children chattered about her, she was off in one of her moods of abstraction. They were used to her periods of "owling about," and they rather enjoyed them. At such times they could more or less do as they pleased— within certain limits. She was neither an overstrict mother nor a "picky" one, but a child relished freedom.

Hattie's imagination had always worked most readily in terms of scenes, and she knew that folk would respond more readily to one deftly drawn picture than to a dozen of the abstractions which William Lloyd Garrison and Wendell Philips and other antislavery orators were hurling into the face of the public. Yes, folk could be moved by graphic pictures of human beings, white as well as black, who were caught in the toils of slavery.

On Sundays she took her family to services in the First
Parish Church across from the Bowdoin campus, where—
among doughty seafarers and pious gentlefolk and college
professors—she sat in a pew as hard-backed and chilly as in
the old Litchfield days. Memories of her girlhood assailed
her as, on one snowy day in February, she prepared to take
communion. It recalled to her that June-time when she
had given herself to Jesus and "He has taken me." And
then there had been the tortured years of doubt and self-
searching until she had come full circle. Again, as at the
age of fourteen, she was able to open her heart fully and
trustfully, not to the Old Testament with its God of
Wrath, but to the New Testament and the love and the
teachings of Jesus.

As she partook of the body and blood of Christ in sym-
bolic ritual on this particular Sunday, she trembled before
a vision so powerful that she choked back her tears. Whatever would the congregation think of Mrs. Calvin Ellis
Stowe if she were to break down in church? No wonder,
poor little soul, with all the troubles she'd seen, they
would say; they would offer her smelling salts and tuck her
into blankets for the short sleigh-ride home.

She was lost in reverie as the twins helped her to set
dinner on the table—transported, still, by her vision. At
last she was able to get away from the household hubbub
and settle down at her desk. What she had seen in church
was the death of an old slave with a magnificent head. His
name must be—there it was—Uncle Tom. A hideous death
caused by the beating of a merciless master, half-brute.
Good and evil—Uncle Tom and Simon Legree.

The psychologist tells of a state, in which the affections
and images of the mind become so dominant and overpower-

ing, that they press into their service the outward senses, and make them give tangible shape to the inward imagining. . . .

Thus Hattie was somewhat able to explain her trance-like state as, with such an inspiration as had never before flooded her whole being, she poured out upon sheet after sheet of the paper spread before her the death of Uncle Tom:

> Scenes of blood and cruelty are shocking to our ear and heart. What man has the nerve to do, man has not nerve to hear. What brother-man and brother-Christian must suffer, cannot be told to us, even in our secret chamber, it so harrows the soul! And yet, oh, my country! these things are done under the shadow of thy laws! O Christ! Thy church sees them, almost in silence!

> But of old, there was One whose suffering changed an instrument of torture . . . into a symbol of glory, honor, and immortal life. . . .

> Was he alone, that long night, whose brave, loving spirit was bearing up, in that old shed, against buffeting and brutal stripes?

> Nay! There stood by him One—seen by him alone—"like unto the son of God." . . .

> Tom opened his eyes, and looked upon his master. "Ye poor miserable critter!" he said, "there an't no more ye can do. I forgive ye, with all my soul!" And he fainted entirely away.

Hattie could see it all before her, as clearly as though it were taking place in her study. The sinister mansion house, Simon Legree's half-crazed but once-beautiful quadroon mistress, the two slaves Sambo and Quimbo who had

hated Tom for his goodness. Fluid descriptions, conversations, characterizations flowed from Hattie's pen hour after
hour until daylight faded and she rose to light the lamp.

Whence had it all come to her, these full-bodied heavy-
breathing portrayals, this narrative that swept all before it
and demanded to be told? When at last, drained but exalted, Hattie summoned her older children to become her
first audience, it was as though she were reading from an
author utterly strange to herself.

Gripped by the story as it enfolded, the childen sat without moving, half-stunned in a silence broken only by their
mother's low voice and the falling of coals in the grate. It
was twelve-year-old Henry who could bear it no longer
and, throwing himself into his mother's arms, cried, "Oh,
mama! Slavery is the cruelest thing in this world." Then
the whole circle broke down and sobbed.

Was the death of Uncle Tom the beginning, the middle,
or the end of what she wished to communicate? It could
not stand alone; of this she was sure as next morning, when
a measure of calm had descended upon her, she ran
through the clear even lines of her fast-moving writing.
Now whatever use could she make of her manuscript?

Readers would be shocked, as her children had been,
shocked and horrified if there were no other pictures to
lead up to this scene and explain it. In the years of her writing, Hattie had become a fair critic; and she knew that
standing by itself the death of Uncle Tom could easily be
put down as a piece of lurid sensationalism that no editor
would accept. It must be surrounded by several other pictures—three or four, but no more than that. She was not a
writer of novels but of sketches, she told herself, as possible
scenes crowded into her mind in such profusion that she
could not decide which to discard.

Fantasy mingled with fact in the endless parade of characters that, like Uncle Tom, were composites. To be sure, he bore a strong resemblance to "Father" Henson; but also he would compare, in faithfulness and loyalty, to the slave husband of a free Negress who had worked for her in Cincinnati. Then, too, Reverend Rankin's account of the miraculous escape across the ice of the Ohio was trying to work itself into her tale.

Often, waking during the night, Hattie wept over the baby son sleeping beside her, thinking of her own good fortune while many a slave mother was desolated. The cruelty and injustice of it all filled her with an anguish that seemed beyond her powers of expression.

Thus tormented, she finally put the disturbing manuscript away into a drawer and did not even tell her husband about it when he arrived early in March. It was not that she had forgotten about it, but that she feared his disapproval which—with her own self-doubts and dismay at the likelihood of being called a female agitator—would likely put an end to her endeavor once and for all.

Yet she had underestimated Calvin Ellis Stowe. Discovering her pages by chance one day, he came to her vainly trying to wipe the tears from his eyes with a handkerchief. She must go on with it, he insisted. Write a novel if that was the form it must take, but go on with it. The Lord had chosen her as His instrument.

18

UNCLE TOM'S CABIN

Cᴀʟᴠɪɴ's ᴇɴᴄᴏᴜʀᴀɢᴇᴍᴇɴᴛ and approval were all that Hattie needed to dash off a letter to the editor of the *National Era* telling him that she was working on a story about slavery that would run longer than any of her previous work; it would be based upon her own observations and those of her friends. She would paint both the best and the worst side of the system, and likely the piece would run through several installments. Was he interested, and what would he pay her?

Three hundred dollars—it seemed a fair sum to Hattie for a serial of the sort she intended. Yes, she could afford to set aside her other work and do it for that, anyway for three or four issues. *Uncle Tom's Cabin, or, Life Among the Lowly. . . .*

In order to arrest the attention of the reader, she would open her tale with an ominous threat of dark happenings and then switch to the supposedly good life she had seen on the Kentucky plantation, to owners who were kind and merciful and yet were caught up in the system. She had never before constructed a novel—and never again would do it as effectively—but now she went about it with instinctive skill. Thus she began one of the most famous novels ever written:

> Late in the afternoon of a chilly day in February, two gentlemen were sitting alone over their wine, in a well-furnished dining parlor. . . . For convenience sake, we have said, hitherto, two *gentlemen*. One of the parties, when critically examined, did not seem, strictly speaking, to come under the species. . . .

With this she launched into a description of that ignoble self-styled "man of humanity," Mr. Haley the slave trader. She had seen many men of his type swaggering about the streets of Cincinnati "much over-dressed, in a gaudy vest of many colors . . . his hands large and coarse . . . plentifully bedecked with rings. . . ." She was depicting a man that her readers would love to hate.

The plantation owner, Colonel Shelby, on the other hand, would be a more sympathetic character, easygoing and good-natured but pressed by his debts. Hattie would show how even the best-intentioned owners were often put into a position where they must sell such a slave as Tom, valued for himself as an individual but still "a man who was a thing." Tom was to be torn from his wife and family and put on the market. And then there was Mrs. Shelby, the most thoughtful and pious of mistresses, who cried out: "This is God's curse on slavery!—a bitter, bitter most accursed thing!—a curse to the master and a curse to the slave! I was a fool to think I could make anything good out of such a deadly evil. . . ."

Hattie was setting out to present the human dilemma

and wisely to point the finger at no one. She knew that
there were thousands of enlightened plantation owners
who felt as did Mrs. Shelby; they were caught in the grip
of a system which was beyond their power to correct. Comparatively few were as brutal and sadistic as Simon Legree,
who would appear later in her story; he would be scorned
and detested by decent men and women wherever they
lived. Above all, Hattie wished to be fair and not permit
her audience to place all the blame on "those southerners"; with an inspiration amounting to genius, she decided
to have Simon Legree hail from New England.

By the end of the first chapter, she had introduced the
engaging child Harry and his beautiful quadroon mother
Eliza, with her delicately formed hand and trim foot. Suspense mounted with the suggestion that Harry, too, was to
be sold to the slave trader. With June of 1851, her story
began to appear weekly in the *National Era,* and immedi-
ately it aroused favorable comment.

By July letters were pouring into the publication praising its rich interest and deep pathos, while Hattie
struggled against the "wind and tide" of household duties
to keep abreast of her deadlines. Each night she read her
day's output to her family and to friends who awaited it
with breathless interest. Even Calvin who "is so nervous,
so afraid of being bored that I feel as if it were something
to hold him" was increasingly absorbed in the tale.

Hattie was on less familiar ground when she decided to
have Tom sold down the river to a cotton plantation in the
Deep South; and accordingly she wrote for information to
Frederick Douglass, the famous Negro orator and abolition
leader. Checking through various documents piling up on
her desk, she somehow was able to keep going because, as
she told a friend later, "I did not write that book." She had
only put down what she saw, she said. ". . . it all came

before me in visions, one after another, and I put them down in words."

Comic relief . . . desperate partings . . . Eliza's escape . . . the angelic child Eva and her father Augustine St. Clare, dashing and cynical, a latter-day translation of Cleon and Hattie's girlish dreams of Lord Byron. He was the son of a father who, instead of staying in New England "to rule over rocks and stones," came to Louisiana "to rule over men and women and force an existence out of them." Slavery—St. Clare was in philosophical mood—"the land groans under it; and, bad as it is for the slave, it is worse, if anything, for the master." For this sensitive man, the treasured memory of his mother—such a mother as Roxana had been—was all he truly respected.

Into the indolent, careless atmosphere of St. Clare's mansion, where Tom was to have a good home, stepped angular Miss Ophelia, cousin to St. Clare; she was the epitome of the New England spinster and "the absolute bondslave of the 'ought.' " Thus, with quick and telling strokes enlivened with wit, Hattie sketched characters that emerged from the page with the full dimensions of actual human beings. Her remarkable memory supplied her with a thousand details which she had noted in passing and which now poured out upon the paper before her as from a subterranean spring. A later generation might explain it by saying that she had been able to make a major breakthrough into the realm of her subconscious mind. Certainly she had cast aside her New England inhibitions to tell a story that placed no censorship upon either violence or debauchery, one that smouldered with elemental passions.

She was sentimental at times, and she could be merry, softening her tale with the antics of Topsy and Miss Ophelia's efforts to turn this sooty gnome who "never was

born, never had no father nor mother, nor nothin' " into a
proper Christian. But she would not have been the daughter of Lyman Beecher had she not thrust an occasional sermon into the mouths of her characters to make certain
points with sarcastic effect.

Hattie had no patience with the slippery double-talking
of many of the clergy who were debasing the true meaning
of Christianity by condoning slavery and claiming that
there were no evils in it not to be found in any other
relation such as marriage or business. Such statements
made her blood boil, and she had St. Clare say in conversa-
tional tones:

> "The whole framework of society, both in Europe and
> America, is made up of various things which will not stand
> the scrutiny of any very ideal standard of morality. It's pretty
> generally understood that men don't aspire after the absolute
> right. . . . Now, when anyone speaks up, like a man, and
> says slavery is necessary to us, we can't get along without it . . .
> this is strong, clear, well-defined language; it has the respect-
> ability of truth to it. . . . But when he begins to put on a
> long face, and snuffle, and quote Scripture, I incline to think
> he's no better than he should be."

Yes, Hattie was sparing no punches. She was speaking
up, and her readers were cheering her on, caring as little as
she did whether what she was writing was literature and
whether it might be classed as realistic or romantic fiction.
That would be for the professors to decide in later years
and for noted authors such as Henry James to marvel how
the little woman had produced a work that seemed to leap
into the air like a natural act of creation.

Often, as Hattie stopped to brush the damp curls from
her forehead, she wondered whether she would have the

stamina to finish or whether, indeed, she could afford to
run on thus long and neglect other sources of income. The
original three or four installments she had planned would
become forty before the work was complete; but despite its
popularity with his readers, the editor was holding her to
his original agreement to pay her but three hundred dollars.

She had never dreamed she had so much to say, or what
threads of plot must be interwoven before they converged
upon the death of Uncle Tom and the final reunion of
Eliza and her child with the husband who had escaped
into Canada. Somber though the tale might be, it must
have a burst of sunshine and hope.

Hattie's only chance of making adequate money out of
Uncle Tom's Cabin was to try to have it brought out in
book form, but she was finding that publishers were exceedingly wary. They feared that sponsoring it might lose
them trade with the South upon all their other titles.
Though Hattie had gone out of her way to be fair and
generous with the southern point of view, still the work
had first appeared in an obscure antislavery weekly. Everyone knew what fanatics those abolitionists were!

Did no book publisher dare to publish *Uncle Tom's
Cabin?* Finally the small Boston firm of Messrs. Jewett &
Co. decided to chance it, but even Mr. Jewett was not
optimistic. He worried as the tale rushed onward into what
could turn out to be hundreds of pages. He was not as
willing to take a gamble upon a book that might have to
go into two volumes—really, Mrs. Stowe must restrain herself! He reminded her that she was writing upon an un-
popular subject and that the general public would not
willingly hear much of it. One short volume at a low price
might possibly sell, but . . .

In reply, Hattie explained that she "did not make the

story, that the story made itself, and that she could not stop until it was done." Calvin sighed; his wife would be lucky if she got enough out of the book to buy herself a length of silk for a dress, he thought. Meanwhile, the bills were piling up, and his small salary could not begin to cover them.

It was almost a year before Hattie was ready to mark "Finis" and lay down her pen. As she did so, "the indignation, the pity, the distress, that had long weighed on her soul seemed to pass off from her." The burden of her own years and of her worries, heartaches, and sorrows had been wrought into the fiber of *Uncle Tom's Cabin;* by writing of injustice and oppression, she too had been liberated. "Blessed are they that mourn, for they shall be comforted. . . ."

The month of March 1852 was blustering when the last weekly installment appeared, and the book was due to appear on the twentieth. As the publisher had feared, he had to bring it out in two volumes and charge the high price of a dollar and a half. Nonetheless, the Boston bookstores were already announcing it, Calvin reported on his return from the metropolis; this seemed to him an excellent portent. He opened a brown paper parcel containing advance copies and handed them on to his wife. Yet, as Hattie held the work in her hand, the work into which she had put "her life-blood, her prayers, and her tears," a feeling of profound discouragement came over her. She had given her best, but in her own words:

Would anybody read it? Would anybody listen? Would this appeal . . . go for nothing, as so many prayers and groans and entreaties of these poor suffering souls had already gone?

She was soon to have an answer so astounding that it was hard for her to believe, she who had been afraid that no one would hear her. Within a few days after publication, *Uncle Tom's Cabin* had sold ten thousand copies, and the news sent her spinning. But this was only the start of a sensation that was sweeping the nation. Nothing like it had ever happened before in the history of American book publishing.

Mr. Jewett was frantic to keep up with the demand as the orders piled higher and higher. Soon he had eight power presses running twenty-four hours a day, with time out only for Sundays. Where it would all end he could not prophesy, nor could the little woman who had started a furor that was spreading to England and France.

Thousands were buying her book and passing it on to an uncounted multitude; thousands were reading it, so gripped by the story that they were unable to put it down until they had finished. Thousands were weeping and wringing their hands—that was what mattered to little Hattie Beecher, who had dared to speak out when others were silent.

In the United States three hundred thousand copies were sold in the first year alone. (Considered in terms of population, a comparable figure in later years would be around a million and a half.) She who had always been bone poor now was suddenly rich. To Hattie and her husband, the first royalty check was a fortune, and others would follow it. Imagine anyone receiving a draft for ten thousand dollars!

19

CELEBRITY

TEN THOUSAND dollars—in the money terms of a later day
it was equivalent to fifty thousand or more. Almost overnight, Hattie Beecher had not only a fortune but fame.
Longfellow and Whittier were praising her, statesmen
were calling *Uncle Tom's Cabin* "the greatest book of the
times," and in France the noted author George Sand was
rhapsodizing:

> Mrs. Stowe is all instinct; it is the very reason that she
> appears to some not to have talent. Has she not talent? What
> is talent? Nothing, compared to genius . . . I cannot say she
> has talent as one understands it in the world of letters, but
> she has genius, as humanity feels the need of genius. . . .
>
> In matters of art there is but one rule, to paint and to
> move. And where shall we find creations more complete,
> types more vivid, situations more touching, more original,
> than in "Uncle Tom". . . ? Honor and respect to you, Mrs.
> Stowe!

Hattie was utterly incredulous of all that was said; it was passing her by like a dream. She was receiving letters of commendation from English lords and, on a trip to New York, was being lionized. Jenny Lind had sent her tickets to a concert which had been sold out for months, choice seats from which to hear the glorious "Swedish Nightingale." Wherever Hattie appeared at receptions and soirées, clinging to the arm of her brother, folk paid more attention to her than to Henry Ward Beecher. It was difficult for Hattie to get used to the fact that she too had become famous. Yet her brother Edward need not be concerned lest praise and notoriety go to her head and "induce pride and vanity." The modest wren was not about to turn into a peacock. To her, it continued to seem odd that crowds wished to see her and to shake her hand. As she remarked wryly, they probably were surprised at her unpretentious appearance and doubtless thought that "God has chosen 'the weak things of this world.' "

But it was not mere happenstance that *Uncle Tom's Cabin* had more impact than any novel ever written. While Hattie Beecher might falter as to art and technique, she was a great storyteller. Instinctively she had gauged the temper of the public, and she had tossed a match into a pile of tinder all ready laid to burn.

What she had done was to personalize the slavery issue. Folk could see it in terms of such chivalrous figures as Augustine St. Clare, such scoundrels as Simon Legree, such profoundly moving situations as those of Eliza and Uncle Tom. She had made it possible for folk to identify with this or that character, and to see slavery not in an abstract way as heretofore, but in terms that were agonizingly human.

At first her novel also sold widely through the South, where plantation owners were grateful to a writer who took her long and thoughtful view and did not unequivocally condemn them. In the persons of St. Clare and Mrs. Shelby she had shown that many were fair, generous, and truly troubled. Yet, as the abolitionists made the most of the abuses she recounted, a reaction began. . . .

Northern businessmen with heavy investments in the cotton business became alarmed at the ever-widening circulation of Hattie's volume of protest; they, too, lived by slavery. It was an institution, a system, in which billions of dollars were at stake. Some claimed, indeed, that fully half of the country's economy was based, in some form, upon it.

Where did this Harriet Beecher Stowe get her facts? Did what she had set down on paper have a grain of truth in it? The disaffected were beginning to whisper and to shout that her novel was pure propaganda.

Though her book was still selling like wildfire in both the United States and abroad, Hattie began to see the ugly side of adulation and fame. Her mail was filled with attacks upon her and her veracity, and one morning she opened an envelope that contained the severed ear of a Negro. The South was suppressing her book until copies were contraband, while northern politicians violently condemned it. It was obvious that they regarded what she had written as "a mine planted at the foundations of the republic, and the fuse was hissing." And it was becoming painfully obvious to Hattie that a friend was wrong when she wrote her that the novel was "going to be the great pacificator that will unite both North and South."

Sectional passions presumably stilled by the Compromise of 1850 flared afresh as, slowly but inexorably, the nation marched on toward a doomsday reckoning. Ten years later, when Hattie visited Abraham Lincoln in the

White House, he was to say to her, "So you're the little woman who started this great Civil War."

He was attempting to be genial, and he must have known that his statement was a vast oversimplification. Forces far beyond the power of any one book to initiate had long been moving toward rupture between the two parts of the nation, a breach that wise men hoped could be avoided by peaceful means, short of war. The pressures were the result of a process of social evolution and growth as the northern industrial giant rose above the waning power of the southern aristocracy. Commerce was pitted against cotton, factories versus planations.

What Hattie had done was to bring the whole problem into brilliant focus and to introduce it to the minds of common men that they might judge for themselves. What she had written was mild by comparison with what she could have exposed. Poring over a mounting mass of documents which she was accumulating in order to prepare a *Key* to *Uncle Tom's Cabin* that would be an answer to those who accused her of misrepresenting the facts, she was filled with cold horror. What she was seeing was an awful indictment of the republic; the legal papers containing reports of trials and court decisions which took up over half of the *Key* were far, far worse than "I supposed or dreamed."

It was a trying time when she needed the consolation of the homely pleasures which now, at long last, she was able to afford. They were moving to Andover, where Calvin Stowe was at last free to accept his appointment; and for the first time his wife, who had endured all manner of inconveniences in previous homes, was having a dwelling remodelled to suit her tastes. Under her watchful eyes, "The Stone Cabin," once a coffin factory, became a cozy pleasant residence with wide welcoming fireplaces to replace the ugly but useful airtight stoves, a home filled with flowering plants and the bright bloom of chintz. Here she could entertain distinguished visitors without apology for how the Stowes had to live.

Despite the astounding and continued success of her first novel, Hattie had no intention whatever of resting upon her oars. She had a second novel with a Maine setting in mind; and in addition to her work on the *Key*, she was writing a newspaper column. The vituperative attacks upon her from many directions sent Calvin into fits of gloom, but the authoress felt herself to be vulnerable only through him. Protected by her deep and abiding faith, she reassured her husband, "Who is he that can harm you if ye be followers of the good?"

Hattie did not lack for either defenders or money. By the end of the bewildering first year after the publication of *Uncle Tom's Cabin*, total world-wide sales were estimated at two and a half million; and in time the book was to be translated into thirty-seven languages. Only the Bible appeared in so many versions. While three Paris newspapers published it, and all Europe was reading it, the book had been pirated abroad; under the loose laws of copyright which then prevailed, she received not a penny for overseas sales. She would take care to protect her later work, but meanwhile she was grateful for this fantastic spread of her message.

She had impressive proof when the most prominent women of Great Britain and Ireland—among them countesses, duchesses, and wives of literary men like Dickens and Tennyson—addressed an appeal to the women of America imploring removal of the "affliction and disgrace" that was slavery. It was a document that bore a half-million signatures from women of all classes.

Furthermore, the antislavery societies of Glasgow were

inviting Hattie and her husband to visit the British Isles
with all their expenses paid. As Hattie raced against time
to get the *Key* off to the publishers, a family party of six
was forming to take "the grand tour." She was having fit-
tings for silk dresses made up with great skirts over crin-
olines in the fashion of the time, but she was not so carried
away as to permit anything but a modesty of lace about the
throat, even for evening. As a New England Puritan, she
was not about to expose neck and shoulders, nor did she
intend to lose her Beecher dignity. Whatever celebrations
their hosts might be planning for them, she would let her
husband take all the bows. As for herself, she was "a little
used-up article . . . dry as a pinch of snuff."

Yet neither of the Stowes could anticipate the enthusiastic adulation which awaited them abroad—what had happened in America was as nothing by comparison. From
their landing in Liverpool they were overwhelmed with
entertainments morning, noon, and night. Often Hattie
was obliged to shut her door and rest in retirement from
the hundreds who clamored to see her, but on the whole
she bore up under it better than Calvin. A tea party for
two thousand guests; crowds lining the streets of Glasgow;
urchins shouting, "That's her; see the *courls!*"; packed
halls in Edinburgh and Aberdeen; gifts pressed upon her
by strangers.

They were trying to do a bit of sight-seeing on the side,
and Hattie was enthralled by the misty beauty of Scotland
and the reminders of Sir Walter Scott before they took
reluctant leave and went on to London.

Famous names were sprinkled thick in the letters she
was writing to her family circle and to friends; they were
filled also with the homely details of her quick and appre-
ciative observation, and they would form the basis of her
next book, *Sunny Memories of Foreign Lands.* She was

hobnobbing with the nobility of England: dinner with
Lord Carlisle, an invitation to the magnificent baronial
home of the Duchess of Sutherland, meetings with Lord
Palmerston and Lord Shaftesbury. She was exhausted, but
her head was not turned; the great were "old shoe" and
easy for her to talk to when she got to know them. Glad-
stone and Macaulay and Lady Byron, so many eminent
folk and such elaborate entertainments that she was reminded of her childhood Thanksgiving days when she was
"plumped down into the midst of pie and pudding."

She was taking time out to flee away to the lovely English countryside, to be amused at the newspaper flurry over
a brown silk dress she was having made. Typically, too, she
paused to consider why English women past fifty remained
in bloom at an age when American women dwindled,
faded, and grew thin. Fresh air and outdoor exercise instead of overheated rooms conducive to indoor indolence
was one answer, but another was the fact that English
women "were not tempted to do the impossible in all
branches which, I believe, is the death of a third of the
women in America." (Speak for yourself, Harriet Beecher
Stowe.)

Truth to tell, the excitement agreed with her, and she
had never looked better than when she posed for an English portrait artist who, with sure strokes of the crayon,
caught the essence of Hattie Beecher at the pinnacle of her
success. She was beautiful, not in the conventional way,
but shining with an inner radiance. Curls fell carelessly
about an oval face with soft full lips and wide glorious
eyes, a face that was all feminine charm. She was the romantic heroine of the fairy tale she was living here in
London. The portraitist was kind to the prominent Beecher nose and the lines of character evident in others of

her portraits, but the flash of her beauty when she was at her best had come through to the artist.

As the feverish round continued, Calvin was often heard to remark with Yankee common sense, "The Lord keep our wits and save our souls!" The climax to their days in London was to be a gigantic antislavery meeting in Exeter Hall with four thousand present; and as Hattie entered to take her seat beside the Duchess of Sutherland, she received an ovation so huge and almost fierce from the mighty mass that it made her tremble. "The hoarse surgings and swellings" were positively frightening. As the speeches began, it was apparent to both her and to Calvin that the meeting was heading toward an anti-American demonstration. The British were using slavery as a weapon to attack the shortcomings of their former colonies and embarrass the United States.

If it was Yankee-baiting that they wanted, Calvin Stowe was ready for them. He was seated across the hall from his wife, and without her hand to restrain him and caution prudence, he rose to his feet. As an assured public speaker, he demanded to know who was responsible for slavery in the United States if it were not Britain itself. Self-righteous, were they? Self-righteous when it was English ships which had profited greatly by the slave trade before it was forbidden? Self-righteous when it was British mills that were using four-fifths of the cotton grown by the slaves?

They could abolish slavery by a single stroke. They could refuse to buy slave-grown cotton. It was that simple.

But—and this was the crux of the matter so far as he was concerned—were they willing to sacrifice a single penny of profit? Moral indignation cost them nothing; and he, for one, did not care for it. Talk . . . talk . . . talk about the conscience of the plantation owner—talk was free. Facing the huge and antagonistic audience, Calvin Stowe himself rose to a height of bravery unusual for him as he thundered, "Has the cotton consumer no conscience? The receiver is as guilty as the thief!"

Hattie had married a man of real stature, and she was mightily proud of him.

With June, Calvin Stowe departed from the indignant atmosphere of London which followed his speech, but it was not a retreat. He had work to do in Andover, and he would leave his wife to explore the Continent with her brother Charles and other members of the party.

It was a tremendous relief for Hattie to become a mere tourist instead of a public figure. No one arranged entertainments for her in Paris, and she was free to love it for its gaiety and, in the Louvre, to study great works of art. There had been no time for that when she was in London. Yes, here was the beauty she had been seeking for all of her life; she was revelling in it amidst the museums of Europe. Strangely enough, of all the masters, the demure little Puritan was to prefer the voluptuous earthly flesh of Rubens, whom she compared to Shakespeare, to an artist like Murillo; she could sense that Murillo was only "most exquisitely reproducing what others had thought."

And then there were the magnificent cathedrals in which she could almost forget her austere Calvinist heritage when, as in Cologne, she "walked with a kind of exultation among those lofty arches, and saw the clouds of incense ascending . . . surely there is some part of man that calls for such a service, for such visible images of grandeur and beauty. . . ."

With a girlishness that belied her forty-two years, she loosened her stays and lifted her skirts to climb over the rocks of the Alps with Charles, revelling in the vibrant wild flowers and skirting the edge of abysses while the others followed on muleback. No expedition seemed too much for her to undertake on this once-in-a-lifetime tour. She would visit Europe again and again in the future, but never with the joy and the exhilaration of these early moments of release from her Puritan bondage.

Just as none of her later books would compare with *Uncle Tom's Cabin*, so this trip to Europe was the height of her lifetime. No family responsibilities, no concern about money, she was intoxicated with these days and these weeks of her freedom.

Back in the States in September, she was soon sitting at a desk that would produce many another work without the tension and uncertainty that had accompanied her writing of *Uncle Tom's Cabin*. She was an established authoress now, and she could count on good sales. She put the Maine novel aside and concentrated upon *Dred: A Tale of the Dismal Swamp*. Her purpose was to show "the general effect of slavery on society; the demoralization of all classes, and the corruption of Christianity which follows in its trail."

While *Dred* was a commercial success, it was disappointing as a sequel to her first novel. She had laid the scene in a mid-South plantation near to the Great Dismal Swamp, and she would be on surer ground in the future with New England backgrounds.

She wrote her third novel as a serial for the newly launched *Atlantic Monthly*, and James Russell Lowell praised it as mastery of her medium. By its sensational aspects, *Uncle Tom's Cabin* had obscured her true genius, he thought; it lay in going "right to the organic elements of human nature, whether under a white skin or a black."

This was *The Minister's Wooing*, and it grew out of twin tragedies. The first was Kate's agony over the loss of her lover years before, when she had been tortured with the concept that his soul was forever damned. The second

was Hattie's own bitter bereavement following the death
of her seventeen-year-old son Henry. A student at Dartmouth, he had been drowned while swimming in the river.
With a desperate need to reconcile herself to his death,
Hattie wrote *The Minister's Wooing*. The Calvinistic
ghost still lurked in the dark corners of her mind; but in
her new book, she exorcised it forever.

Its theme was revolt against the cruel God of eighteenth
century Calvinism, the God of Fear who chose few for
salvation. Again, as with Uncle Tom, Hattie chose a Negro
to express her own religious beliefs. She had black Candace
say, "Why, Jesus didn't die for nothin'—all dat love a'n't
gwine to be wasted . . . ef tings was as some folks suppose, why, we couldn't live, and dar wouldn't be no sense
in anything dat goes on. . . ."

Her Maine novel, long dormant in her mind, would
come later—*Pearl of Orr's Island*. And then there would be
Oldtown Folks, which was not in reality a novel but a
series of sketches based upon the quaint characters which
Calvin had known in his boyhood. Like *Poganuc People*—
written toward the end of Hattie's career as an idealization
of her own girlhood—it was a penetrating and often delightful and amusing regional study that was to give rise to
a whole school of New England novelists.

In between these most significant of her works, many
another volume appeared; Hattie was facile, and her output was prodigious. Almost every year witnessed the appearance of a book that bore her name—collections of
stories and articles, tales for children. She was moving on
terms of close friendship with the leading literary folk of
her day: Oliver Wendell Holmes, the Hawthornes, George
Eliot, John Ruskin, the Brownings.

Through urgent necessity, she had become the family
money-maker; and Calvin, with his professor's stipend, en-

joyed spending it as much as she did. They were almost childlike, to the consternation of sister Mary's lawyer-husband, who had become Hattie's financial advisor. Hattie was as generous to others as she was to her own family, giving large sums to free slaves, to Negro education, and to other philanthropies, as though the shower of gold had no limit.

What with her sadness over her young son's untimely death and her concern with other problems, it was well that Hattie had "sunny memories" with which to fortify herself as the nation moved toward the "irreconcilable conflict." Had she been a person of less common sense and less humility, she might have been tormented by the role which *Uncle Tom's Cabin* had played. There was no gainsaying the fact that her book had done nothing to ease a tense situation and that it had played upon emotions until the characters she created had become a national myth.

Dramatized for the stage in hundreds of versions over which she had no control and for which she received no royalties, her story had been distorted and cheapened beyond all recognition. Travelling road shows playing to the small towns and villages had made a good thing out of it. Little Eva ascended to heaven and became an angel swinging from ropes; Topsy put on the plug hat of a minstrel; and hounds pursued Eliza enthusiastically across the ice. It had become a folk drama; and in the course of the transformation, *Uncle Tom's Cabin* suffered severely. It was ironical that in years to come the book which Hattie Beecher had written as a plea for freedom and justice should be twisted by various interpretations so that "Uncle Tom" gradually became a symbol of servility scorned by others of his race.

As the Civil War darkened the sky and filled every household with gloom and foreboding, Hattie was writing, always writing. Dread news filled the papers, but valiantly she was trying to keep up her own spirits and those of her household with "a little general household merriment and talk of common things." She had her personal sorrows along with those of the nation when her son Frederick was struck by a fragment of shell at Gettysburg and, presumably as the result of his wound, was to become a serious problem that she and Calvin tried in vain to solve until he disappeared and was never heard from again.

Seated at her desk, Hattie was joining many another to urge immediate emancipation for the slaves that the fearful loss of life might not be in vain. She was in the Boston Music Hall when the news came that Lincoln had finally signed the Emancipation Proclamation. The crowd called her name; and appearing over the edge of the balcony, she wept into her handkerchief.

It was as a distraction from the bloody war and as a fulfillment of a girlish dream that upon Calvin's retirement from Andover she started building a great house that was to be an extravagance of Victorian architecture. She had bought acres in Hartford in the beautiful grove along the river where she and her beloved Georgianna had wandered as schoolgirls, and here she who had been starved for beauty would surround herself with her idea of the best. The house would have eight gables, rich oak panelling, and an Italian fountain playing in the midst of a two-story conservatory visible from her study and from the entrance hall.

Though the house would never be entirely finished because of the fast-mounting costs, she soon was hurrying to get the mansion into a shape that would serve as impressive background for a wedding. The twins, her first-born, had waltzed all over Europe but had brought back no suitors; it was vivacious Georgie who was to be married.

No expense was being spared for this first daughter's launching. She was to embark like a princess upon the matrimonial sea, as the wedding gifts indicated: "every kind of silver thing that can be conceived" and a bridegroom's present of five strands of real pearls clasped with diamonds. There were moments when Hattie must have remembered her own start in married life with eleven dollars for china.

It had been long ago and far away. Now little Hattie Beecher was rich with living and rich with achievement. It had been a long road and a hard road; but even when submerged by her cares and her sorrows, she had seldom admitted defeat. In his odd and fumbling way, Calvin had helped her. He had given her children whom she could love with all of her heart, given her life purpose and meaning which she had further fulfilled with her pen.

Now that the years were moving on for both of them, he wore a black skullcap, and she called him "old Rab"; he had long been inclined toward Judaism where she favored the Episcopalian church. Increasingly birdlike, Hattie reached the time when she longed to rest. There came the time when she felt like the woman "who always was tired, 'cause she lived in a house where help wasn't hired." Whimsically, she went on with the verse:

She folded her hands with the latest endeavor
Saying nothing, dear nothing, sweet nothing forever.

Hattie was to live to be eighty-five, but on her seventieth birthday she made her last appearance before a large audience. It was on the occasion of a great garden party given in her honor by the *Atlantic Monthly*. Poems written to her by Holmes, Whittier, and many another called attention to her natural gifts which amounted to genius. In her quiet, modest way and yet in a strong clear voice, she thanked them:

"And one thing more,—that is, if any of you have doubt, sorrow or pain, if you doubt about this world, just remember that this great sorrow of slavery has gone, gone by forever."

Her century was almost over when she died on July 1, 1896, but she had made a mighty mark upon it. Read over a hundred years later out of the sound and the fury of her times, *Uncle Tom's Cabin* still stands as a truly great novel and a great picture of an age and a nation.

BIBLIOGRAPHY

Beach, Seth Curtis: *Daughters of the Puritans,* Boston, American Unitarian Association, 1905.

Beals, Carleton: *Our Yankee Heritage,* New York, McKay, 1955.

Beard, Charles A. and Mary R.: *The Rise of American Civilization,* New York, Macmillan, 1936, rev. ed.

Brooks, Van Wyck: *Flowering of New England 1815–1865,* New York, Dutton, 1936.

Clements, Colin and Ryerson, Florence: *Harriet,* New York, Scribner, 1943.

Cross, Barbara M. ed.: *Autobiography of Lyman Beecher,* 2 vols., Cambridge, Harvard University Press, 1961.

Erskine, John: *Leading American Novelists,* New York, Holt, 1910.

Fields, Annie, ed.: *Life and Letters of Harriet Beecher Stowe,* Boston, Houghton, 1897.

Foster, Charles H.: *The Rungless Ladder,* Durham, Duke University Press, 1954.

Furnas, J. C.: *Goodbye to Uncle Tom,* New York, Sloane, 1956.

Gilbertson, Catherine: *Harriet Beecher Stowe,* New York, Appleton-Century, 1937.

Hibben, Paxton: *Henry Ward Beecher: An American Portrait,* New York, Doran, 1927.

Howard, Joseph: *Life of Henry Ward Beecher,* Philadelphia, Hubbard, 1887.

Johnston, Johanna: *Runaway to Heaven, New York,* Doubleday, 1963.

Wilson, Edmund: *Patriotic Gore,* New York, Oxford, 1962.

Wilson, Forrest: *Crusader in Crinoline,* Philadelphia, Lippincott, 1941.

Stowe, Charles Edward: *Life of Harriet Beecher Stowe,* compiled from her Letters and Journals, Boston, Houghton, 1889.

Stowe, Charles Edward and Stowe, Lyman Beecher: *Harriet Beecher Stowe,* Boston, Houghton, 1911.

Stowe, Harriet Beecher: Letters in the Huntington Library Collection, San Marino, California.

Stowe, Harriet Beecher: *The Minister's Wooing,* New York, Burt, 1859.

Stowe, Harriet Beecher: *Oldtown Folks,* Boston, Fields, 1869.

Stowe, Harriet Beecher: *Poganuc People,* London, Sampson Low, 1879.

Stowe, Harriet Beecher: *Sunny Memories of Foreign Lands,* Boston, Phillips, 1854.

Stowe, Harriet Beecher: *Uncle Tom's Cabin,* Boston, Jewett, 1852.

Stowe, Lyman Beecher: *Saints, Sinners and Beechers,* Indianapolis, Bobbs-Merrill, 1934.

INDEX

THE AUTHOR

Since her graduation from the University of Wisconsin, WINIFRED E. WISE has spent her entire career in writing in one form or another. She has been a newspaper reporter and feature writer, a staff editor of *Compton's Pictured Encyclopedia,* a copywriter in retail stores and advertising agencies and an advertising executive with Marshall Field & Company. Miss Wise has also written six biographies (including this one) and six novels, and is presently working on a biography of Fanny Kemble to be published by Putnam. She is the former wife of Stuart Palmer, the mystery author, has three children in their twenties, and lives near the ocean in Laguna Beach, California.